Diderot's Chaotic Order

Lester G. Crocker

Diderot's Chaotic Order

Approach to Synthesis

Princeton University Press
1974

Published by Princeton University Press
Princeton and London

LCC: 73-22127
ISBN: 0-691-07199-3

Library of Congress Cataloging in Publication
Data will be found on the last printed page of this book

Publication of this book has been aided by the Whitney Darrow
Publication Reserve Fund of Princeton University Press

This book has been composed in Linotype Baskerville

Printed in the United States of America by
Princeton University Press
Princeton, New Jersey

for Billie, and for Roger,
Leslie and Fred

*Sunt lacrymae rerum et mentem
mortalia tangunt*

Contents

Preface

ORDER AND DISORDER ARE FUNDAMENTAL categories of our experience and our modes of thought. Whether they are subjective forms of apprehending and interpreting experience or perceptions of objective relationships is not easy to decide. They undoubtedly have affective aspects and are related to our security and our needs. However, although ideas of good order, or even of order itself, are quite variable, there are surely objective correlatives of these ideas, for instance in physical and social phenomena. No one—to take extreme examples—would consider a destructive hurricane or a war to be forms of order. Yet one could argue that the one is intrinsic to the physical laws of what is called "the natural order," and that war, like revolution, is also a violent process of replacing one order by another, conceivably a better one. This is the inescapable ambiguity that makes the subject difficult to deal with, both for the philosopher and for the scholar who wishes to understand the philosopher.

The ancient Hebrews were probably more impressed by cosmic disorder than by order. Yahweh was a God of justice, and he was intended to be an ordering principle; but the Book of Job reveals a deep apprehensiveness on the part of thinking men in a God-centered culture. Even if God had created an orderly world, there was no doubt that men were constantly discomposing it, thereby inciting His wrath. Disorder was even more vividly present in the mind of the Greeks. Zeus was unable to govern his unruly gods, and the Greeks, at least in literature, exploited the traditional rivalries among the deities by calling on one or the other for protection. It was man's task, the philosophers held, to build an order, but they did not succeed. The social and political world, in both areas, was turbulent.

One of Christianity's great contributions, and a preeminent feature of the vast cultural revolution it produced, was the security of a stable, rationally satisfying and benign cosmic order in which people could and did believe. Men's lives, in their social and moral aspects, were no better than before, but the weight of this disorder was lightened by the certainty that this transitory world would be superseded by the order of the life eternal to which it was the ordained passage, as well as by the hope engendered by various millennial prophetic schemes.[1]

The great step from the closed world to the infinite universe, as Alexandre Koyré called it, was the second major revolution in the history of Western civilization. The effects of the dissolution of the Christian synthesis have not yet been absorbed or remedied. The loss of the bases for order, and the resulting insecurities, represents the furthest reach of a complex of causes that lies at the root of the present crisis of Western civilization and of all the plans that have been advanced for a new way in which men can live, and live together. The critical outburst of this problem, its first explosive and

[1] Frank E. and Fritzie P. Manuel, "Sketch for a Natural History of Paradise," *Daedalus*, vol. 101 (1972), pp. 83-128.

pervasive impact, came in the period usually called the Enlightenment.[2]

An adequate account of these developments cannot be given here. It may, however, be useful to recall certain prominent signposts.

Bayle could be characterized as the great revealer of disorder, in the cosmos and among men. All evidences of order are dissolved in the acid of his corrosive skepticism. Both God and men are convicted of conniving in evil. One particular dimension he introduced was the realm of history, which he saw as a meaningless web of disorderly events.

The name of Fontenelle is traditionally coupled with Bayle's as initiators of the Enlightenment. On this subject Fontenelle's scientific interests led him down a different path. A more smiling skepticism looked more tolerantly on human disorder, while the advances of astronomy made him the exponent of law and order in the physical universe.

Montesquieu's particular interest lay in the sphere of political behavior and organization. Combining history and the present scene, he found the materials he needed to support and illustrate the laws that inhere in the various types of political ordering of societies and which, if observed, would enhance their stability.

Voltaire was the worthy successor to Bayle. While he did not equal Bayle's erudition and razor-sharp logic, he had other qualities that made him a man of first rank. Among these was a heart that enabled him to intuit the depths of the human predicament and to feel deeply about it. Only in a superficial sense can he be

[2] See L. G. Crocker, *An Age of Crisis* and *Nature and Culture*, Baltimore, 1959, 1963.

called superficial. In his grasp of this central problem of Western man, he was the most profound writer of the century. The whole problem of disorder receives a broad and inclusive treatment at his hands, embracing God and cosmos, history, politics, morals, law, interpersonal relationships. While his specific answers may often be qualified as shallow, because he found the issues too difficult to cope with, his acute feeling for the problem helped to crystallize it, to make it both an intellectual and an emotional issue.

Rousseau, on the other hand, was able to dispose rather easily of the problem in its cosmic aspects (God, the universe, man's place, the moral conscience). His famous letter to Voltaire (August 18, 1756) in answer to the *Poème sur le désastre de Lisbonne* and the *Profession de foi* are sufficient evidence. The problem of human order and disorder, however, took on new dimensions and new depths as he penned the most radical and profound critique of society ever written, and as he sketched the outlines of a true society and the methods of remaking man into a truly social being. Although his influence has worked in contradictory directions, and the meaning of his work is still hotly contested, there is little doubt that he is the most original and seminal—in a word, the most important—thinker of the age.

Where does Diderot stand? His feeling of cosmic anguish before "the human predicament" falls short of Voltaire's, and he lacks the sense of a broad historical perspective on the human adventure. His insight into political theory, social problems, and anthropology, and the originality of his thought in these fields, do not even stand comparison with Rousseau's, though many will think his ideas to be saner and more palatable. And yet, in several ways, his approach to the general problem of order and disorder is more significant and exciting than those of Voltaire, Rousseau, or of any one else in the eighteenth century. He had a clearer and firmer conception of the problem as a problem, and he held it constantly before himself. None of his writings sets out to solve the question, but it suffuses almost everything he approached. It is the substance and the mode of all other problems. In his inquiries into the cosmic, into the moral life, into politics, he follows lines undreamed of by Voltaire or Rousseau, in their own way at least as significant. To these he adds the new dimension of aesthetics. Finally, it was typical of his intuitive, exploratory mind both to find relationships among these several spheres and to uncover the paradoxes and complexities that are inherent in the problem. He will not offer us simple or systematic answers, but rather an unsurpassed understanding, the result of his uncompromising intellectual courage and his openmindedness.

Diderot's philosophy has been studied by many outstanding scholars, always analytically. They have analyzed either the growth of his thought, from work to work, or else a particular aspect of his philosophy—science, aesthetics, and so on. The range of his concerns and the dispersed, rather chaotic expression of his ideas that is so characteristic of him have seemed to defy a synthetic approach, which has been possible in the case of Rousseau. While one cannot, when writing about an author as much studied as Diderot, avoid going over some ground already traversed, the novel approach that is taken here will, it is hoped, enable us to gain new insights and especially to reach a synthetic grasp of his thought. Analysis cannot of course be avoided; and other paths to a synthesis are doubtless possible. However, the question of order and disorder has the breadth and depth, the universality and centrality in Diderot's thought for it to be singularly effective.

It would be desirable to go further. A wider study of the Enlightenment from the viewpoint of the problems of order and disorder is needed. The contribution of this inquiry is necessarily limited, but it will hopefully be suggestive.

Diderot's Chaotic Order

I.
Cosmic Order

THE UNIVERSE, FOR DIDEROT, IS MATTER and process. Any static or synchronic conceptualization, even including motion and its laws, is inadequate, although these mechanical phenomena are basic elements on which change and "le devenir" ("becoming") depend. The shift to a diachronic universe has momentous consequences. It is the offspring of Descartes and Leibniz, rather than of the Christian or the Newtonian world-views, and was reinforced by the nascent but powerful notion of geological and biological evolution. It calls renewed attention to the problem of order. While none of the previous theological and moral components is lost, the problem now acquires new metaphysical dimensions, precisely in regard to the nature of process, that is, of the cosmic processes that were being discovered. Obviously, both the physical and the biological are involved, and one of Diderot's merits is to have perceived their ultimate inseparability.

The boundaries of the problem, in Diderot's mind, are the contradictory coexistence of law and the turbulent workings of law. This highly paradoxical and unsolvable antinomy constitutes not only the base of the problem but the circle in which his thought wanders, in apparently uncertain and contradictory fashion. It will become clear, I hope, that the apparent contradictions are only restatements of the problem itself and are contained in its very nature.

Diderot did not see all its aspects at once. Its dimensions grew as he advanced from one problem to another or reached different stages of his thought. He glimpsed the universality of its import from the very beginning, however.

The *Pensées philosophiques* (1746) is concerned with disputes about religious and cosmic questions. Yet it begins with a conventional defense of the passions, typical of the *morale laïque* that was being held up against Christianity, but at the same time quite unconventional when viewed against the problem of order. In a romantic, almost rebellious tone, Diderot exalts the passions as the free exercise of energy without which greatness is impossible. Intrinsically disorderly because unrestrained, they are nonetheless useful and necessary. Establishing his point in four of the five Pensées devoted to the subject, he undoes it in the remaining one (Pensée IV), in which he argues that the passions will be harmless only as long as they are in "harmony" among themselves; in that case, "do not fear any disorders from them."[1] The discipline and self-domination required for such a harmony contradicts the central point of the argument (Pensée III): "Constraint annihilates the greatness and energy of nature" (*mutatis mutandis,* "of the soul").

The analogy of the passions of the soul (to use Descartes' phrase) and the energy of nature is prolonged in the description of a beautiful and useful tree. In Diderot's synthetic, analogy-seeking mode of thought, the basic question, at this point, is the same for man and for nature. Both are characterized by energy. Its

[1] Diderot, *Oeuvres philosophiques,* ed. P. Vernière, Paris (1956), p. 11. References will be to this edition unless otherwise noted.

effects, when restrained only by an inner harmony, are aesthetically satisfying and physically beneficial. The criteria are entirely anthropocentric and subjective.

We can see that Diderot is only nibbling at the edges of a vast problem; but the points he makes will acquire amplitude and significance.

He reaches deeper ground in the dialogue between the atheist and the deist that begins in Pensée XV. The argument mingles two problems which are not necessarily the same: the origin of the known universe and the character of its processes. The motion of particles may have engendered this world, the atheist contends, even though he cannot explain how. Admitting it is a world of orderly process, he is compelled to hold up the moral and human sphere ("the disorders that rule the moral sphere"), and to fall back on Bayle's famous paradox of God's "impuissance ou mauvaise volonté." At this stage of his life, Diderot was still a deist, but he was fighting a losing battle. In making the world into a self-regulating machine, the disciples of both Descartes and Newton were only one step away from atheism, even though the latter required God for occasional repairs and adjustments.

The deist's defense now proceeds to the firmer terrain of biology. First, the origin of life is inexplicable without a special entity, germ cells. If the motions of particles can perhaps explain the physical order, they cannot explain life, only what develops from what is already living. Life, then, represents an ordering designed by God (Pensée XIX). It is not producible by processes characterized by chance. Living organisms are the passive and static products of God's design. In the deist's mind, then, temporal processes are not a real factor in the cosmos. The world is "a machine which has its wheels, its cords, pulleys, springs and weights" (Pensée XVIII). Second, the clear evidences of adaptation to function, as in the wing of a butterfly, are a crushing witness to the workings of a divine intelligence (Pensée XX).

In his rebuttal (Pensée XXI), the atheist removes the original ordering of the world ("this order that astounds you") from the realm of intelligence to the simple mechanical motions of particles arranging themselves strictly according to chance, or the calculus of probability. There is no effort to explain why particles combine or form themselves into an order. The idea of process, however, is introduced by the atheist when he speaks of "those admirable orderings in the infinite multitude of orderings nature has successively taken on." This is the first evidence of what will be a dominant theme in Diderot's cosmic conception: a dynamic universe in which catastrophism is the dramatic motor.[2] The implication is one of a succession of orders. The unasked and unanswered question is whether each order, each universe, is part of an ultimate meta-order or a meta-disorder. To the deist, on the other hand, the world appears as a harmony—at least the physical world.

A slight progression can be noted in Diderot's thinking when, the following year, he writes *La Promenade du sceptique.* If he is no longer enchanted by the idea of a finalistic, beneficent deity, he still is inclined to attribute the undeniable order in biological teleology to a divine intelligence. In the sentence, "the sky darkened; a thick cloud hid nature's spectacle from us," Jacques Roger astutely sees "a curious portent of the

[2] See Colm Kiernan, "Additional Reflections on Diderot and Science," *Diderot Studies XIV*, pp. 116, 134 *et passim.*

Lettre sur les aveugles."[3] Roger concludes that the importance of this work lies in its turning away from the whole question of the proofs of God's existence, and in its reducing "the entire metaphysical debate to the single problem of order in nature."

The complexities and confusions of the problem burst into full view in Diderot's first major work, the *Lettre sur les aveugles* (1749). Diderot's intention is to "banish mysteries," substituting the laws of nature for them. Law implies order, at least at the operational level. Yet the very method he uses involves an explicit admission of disorder—not necessarily of a meta-disorder, but at the operational level itself. (This conflict formed the nub of the question of evil, which tormented eighteenth-century minds; but Diderot is not concerned with it for its own sake.) The problem is now approached through pathology and teratology. Only by taking the viewpoint of the disordered—here that of Saunderson, the man who was born blind (actually, he was blinded from smallpox at twelve months)—can we glimpse the true character of what we conventionally call the order of the world. Here the subjective element in our apprehension of existents as an order, with all its implications of sensory experience, intellectual need, and aesthetic satisfaction, is given full sway for the first time. Saunderson's perceptions and reactions are very different from those of the sighted.[4]

We need recall only the pertinent ideas in Saunder-

[3] J. Roger, *Les Sciences de la vie dans la pensée française du XVIIIe siècle*, Paris, 1963, p. 590.

[4] *Oeuvres philosophiques*, p. 93 *et seq*. "But this confusion between the *order* and the *beauty* of nature is revealing. It shows the importance of emotion, both aesthetic and moral, in the deism Diderot had professed until then." (J. Roger, *op. cit.*, p. 591.)

son's fictitious death-bed disquisition.[5] The dying mathematician does not deny the marvelous order of the human body, despite his infirmity, but only the unwarranted extrapolation to an intelligent and finalistic universal order. Instead, he takes an unexpected and dramatic tack. As a Newtonian, he must concede that the universe is an order. As the voice of Diderot, for whom time, becoming, and the life-sciences were opening new vistas into the problem, he goes beyond Newtonian positivism and boldly enters the realm of cosmic speculation.

The poetic vision harks back to Lucretius: a primal chaos that (for unexplained reasons) became organized into living forms, specifically into animals. If we may assume that this process was governed by laws inherent to matter (though it is not so stated), then those laws depend on a large element of what can only be called chance, and not on intelligent design. Most combinations formed in the initial upheaval were, apparently, unviable "monsters." Only a few were able to survive. We have, then, a dynamic nature, whose built-in "finalities" are its own operational laws. Time is a relatively unimportant factor in this process, as Diderot conceived of it in 1749. He emits a kind of "big-bang" hypothesis, an essentially single event of formation and subsequently a general "cleansing" ("dépuration") of the newly established order. After this primal departure, process of course continues, but only within the general order. Even on this level, order frequently breaks down and monsters—such as Saunderson himself—are not uncommon.

Time is important, however, if we take an even longer view. Why should we not extend the notion of a

[5] *Oeuvres philosophiques*, pp. 118-24.

hit-and-miss process from the products of the existing universal order to that order itself? Why assume that the creation of a universe is a unique event? The same governing factor of chance should lead us to conclude that infinite space, containing an infinite quantity of matter that is everywhere subject to inherent laws of "motion"—we now have an explanation, purely mechanistic, of universal process—is constantly forming universes, many of which are as unviable as the particular products of our own viable universe.

> What is this world, monsieur Holmes? A compound subject to revolutions, all of which point to a continuous tendency to destruction; a rapid succession of beings which follow one another, push each other aside and disappear; a fleeting symmetry; a momentary order.[6]

This statement provides the key to the process itself. All orders are not only imperfect, they are temporary. "Motion continues and will continue to combine accumulations of matter, until they have achieved some structure (*arrangement*) in which they can subsist." On the other hand, we also have the "revolutions" and the continual tendency to destruction. Diderot's concept of universal process consists, then, of a basic dualism, an endless struggle between two opposing dynamic forces.[7] Energy and change are the very essence of mat-

[6] Ibid., p. 123.

[7] The importance of change, becoming, and permanence of the whole have been commented on in various recent writings. See, for instance, Arnolds Grava, "Diderot and Recent Philosophical Trends," *Diderot Studies IV*, p. 76, and Colm Kiernan, *loc. cit.* I should disagree with Grava's interpretation of the aspect of permanence from the viewpoint of totality (p. 100); only the amount of matter and energy is permanent, for Diderot.

ter, which is all that exists. But they operate in two opposite ways. There is, to use anthropomorphic terms, a constant search for structure, order, stability—and, simultaneously, a constant breakdown and increase in disorder, involving the same energy. In modern terms, all existence is a "struggle" against increasing entropy, an "effort" or tendency to persist in organized forms. This is, and will remain, Diderot's fundamental view of being. This is the eternal ontological law. It obtains on both the macrocosmic and the microcosmic levels, in the world we know and in all the other worlds about which we can only speculate. Other natural laws may change, as one order disappears and another comes into being. In this sense, what we call science is temporary and illusory. This law alone is as eternal as matter itself: the disorderly efforts to construct and to maintain an order, and the inevitable destruction of this precarious stability. It is not in itself a dialectic, at least on the general or cosmic level, since there is no solution or transformation of the endless antagonism, or of its outcome, the perpetual making and unmaking of convolutions.

These causative factors of process bring about an order which contains much disorder. The reason for this consequence is precisely the absence of design; put in another way, it is the randomness, which we call "chance," that coexists with what seems to us to be law, or causal determinism. Such randomness is not contradictory to determinism or to cause-effect on a statistical basis, and the theory of probability is the one aspect of mathematics in which Diderot continued to have faith.[8]

[8] See *Le Rêve de d'Alembert*, ed. J. Varloot, Paris, 1962, p. LXX, and *Oeuvres*, III, 456, IX, 192.93, XII, 211. See also the article "Jouer" in the *Encyclopédie*. A contemporary physicist,

That which is not strictly predictable, and answers to no conceived purpose or plan, even though it is caused (as every event is in some way), may be called chance. Disorder is, then, associated both with the process itself and with its products, whether these be judged in terms of success or, on a quite different basis, in terms of human evaluation and appreciation.

The foregoing conception of universal process implies universal energy, conceived in mechanical terms as motion, and constituting a ceaseless dynamism. Diderot was to give a theoretical basis to his theory much later, in 1770, in the *Principes philosophiques sur la matière et le mouvement*. Two postulates are involved. One is the denial of an earlier, Cartesian or Spinozist mechanistic philosophy, according to which matter is homogeneous substance, qualities or attributes not being essential to its definition. On the contrary, Diderot maintains, matter is particulate and heterogeneous, though none the less governed by mechanical laws. Each "molecule" has a different motion, or energy. This fact accounts for the heterogeneity of matter.[9] Continuity, or the ultimate unity of nature, both synchronic and diachronic, is accounted for by development governed by law. The second postulate is (to state it in more modern terms) that motion is only a visible or kinetic form of energy (Diderot uses the words "action" and "force"). Energy

J. M. Jauch, explains that deterministic cause and chance coexist in all dynamically unstable systems; even Newtonian mechanics *contains something like an uncertainty principle*. This view of modern science, which is very close to Diderot's, is not typical of materialist doctrine. See J. M. Jauch, *Are Quanta Real? A Galilean Dialogue*, "Second Day."

[9] M. Wartofsky, "Diderot and the Development of Materialist Monism," *Diderot Studies II*, pp. 301-304.

is present in all matter; if it does not, as in the modern view, constitute the essence of matter (more precisely, the two are equivalent), it is at least essential to it.

> By itself, by the nature of its essential qualities, a body whether it is considered as molecules or as a mass, is full of action and force. . . . The molecule, endowed with the specific quality (characteristic) of its nature, is an active force by itself. . . . Absolute rest is an abstract notion that does not exist in nature. . . . The inner force of the molecule is inexhaustible. It is immutable, eternal. . . . An atom moves the world.[10]

These two principles make the cosmic process possible:

> But I fix my eyes on the general accumulation of bodies. I see everything in action and reaction; everything becoming decomposed in one form; everything restructuring itself in another form: sublimations, dissolutions, combinations of all kinds, phenomena incompatible with the homogeneity of matter. Whence I conclude that it is heterogeneous; that an infinity of different elements exist in nature; that each of these elements, by virtue of its distinctness, has its own force, innate, immutable, eternal, indestructible; and that these forces contained in bodies exert action outside of themselves. From all this results the motions or rather the general ferment in the universe.[11]

The last sentence recalls a formulation in the *Lettre sur les aveugles*, "In the beginning, when matter in ferment brought forth the universe."[12] We must avoid the

[10] *Oeuvres philosophiques*, pp. 394-96.

[11] Ibid., p. 398.

[12] Ibid., p. 123.

error of always taking the word "*fermentation*" in its chemical sense, which it sometimes has; it is often a metaphoric expression of the turbulence of matter in motion, and is more accurately rendered as "ferment." It is not opposed to mechanism, but rather to creationism.

Diderot further clarified his thought in the article "Chaos," which appeared in November 1753 in the third volume of the *Encyclopédie*, but was undoubtedly composed many months earlier. The article is written in a tone of transparent antiphrasis, seemingly from a Christian viewpoint, but Diderot's own opinions can be rather easily disengaged from it. The ancient philosophers, he declares, explained the formation of the universe from an original chaos of "particles of all kinds," by the motions that were essential to them. The Stoics conceived of cosmic history as a succession of such emergences from chaos, culminating in that combination which created the stability of our own universe. Diderot refers to Dr. Thomas Burnet,[13] purposely distorting the import of his theory, to support the idea that the earth was originally formless. The water that, according to Moses, then covered the earth, was not really water, but a kind of slime, whose "fermentation" through time produced the earth in its present form. The same idea is enlarged, in startlingly modern terms: "movement (motion) gradually brought forth, by internal fermentation, collapses, attractions, a sun, an earth. . . ."[14] Ironically, Diderot pretends to prefer the physics of Moses, which stipulates constant, universal

[13] *Sacred Theory of the Earth* (*Telluris Theoria Sacra*), 1681-89.

[14] Diderot, *Oeuvres complètes*, ed. Assezat-Tourneux, Paris, 1875-77, vol. XIV, p. 90.

laws as an explanation of the conservation of the created universe, but not of its formation by a process of blind mechanical motion.

Diderot's principal published work of scientific speculation, *De l'Interprétation de la nature*, appeared in the same month as the article "Chaos," and in a revised version in January 1754. A lapse of time between this work and the article is indicated by the more advanced state of his theorizing. It is characterized by a major shift to the biological and by emphasis on the limits of the mind as it delves into ultimate questions.

One aspect of these limits is expressed in Diderot's rejection of the mathematical approach (Pensées II, III). He attacks mathematics on the basis of its lack of a necessary relation with physical reality. Mathematics represents an intellectual, self-contained order, peculiar to the human mind. The natural order (whether we call it an order or a disorder remains to be determined), can be deduced only from experimental evidence. From what he says a bit later, it appears that the chief lack of correspondence lies not only in what he considers to be the conventional and circular nature of mathematical proof, but in the immutable, static character of the truths it develops. It is an order created by the needs and the mode of operation of the intellect.

The next important point, in this series of disconnected speculations, is the assertion of the unknowability of "the universal mechanism" (Pensée VI). This is posited as a fundamental and impenetrable barrier, because it is a limit of mind itself. Like Voltaire in *Micromégas,* Diderot contends that, even if God had written out a complete explanation, it would be incomprehensible to us. Unlike *Micromégas,* whose blank page suggests an absurd world in which there is really nothing to understand by any rational process, Diderot believes in "the great chain that links all things," and does not doubt an order consisting of universal laws and the interplay in the world that results from it.

This conviction is given positive statement later on (Pensée XXXVI, para. 2). "Chaos is an impossibility; for there is an order that is essentially consistent with (*or,* consequent to) the primitive qualities of matter." In this formulation, already adumbrated by La Mettrie, "essentially" is the key word. It not only places science and scientific speculation on a purely naturalistic basis, but its implication of necessity entails a deterministic universe, but quite possibly one without intelligent design or acceptable order in human terms. As J. Roger puts it: "Immutability, which nonetheless relates only to the *ensemble,* for the particular systems that compose it react endlessly and ceaselessly on each other."[15]

Diderot's thinking is by now not so vague as his formulation—actually a concluding induction in his text—would make it seem. Two molecules that attract each other, he explains, will compose an arrangement: "each will determine the other in a spatial relationship, according to the laws of their attraction, their shape, etc." The same result obtains with a plurality of particles, which will eventually form a "system." The characteristic of any system is its resistance to what we call increasing entropy, or to what Diderot would call disorder. The factor he terms "essential" is again the tendency to "seek" stable formations and to maintain them against an equally essential counterforce that tends to decompose viable structures which (we should say) depend on an effective organization of energy-systems. It is perhaps not going too far beyond Diderot's

[15] J. Roger, *op. cit.,* p. 609.

possibilities of conceptualization to assume that in his own primitive way, he was thinking of structures as self-regulating systems of transformation.

> . . . they will resist a force that tends to disturb their coordination, and will always tend either to return to their original ordering, if the perturbing force happens to cease, or to restructure their arrangement according to the laws of their attraction, their shape, etc., and according to the action of the perturbing force, if it continues to act. This system A is what I call an elastic body. In this general and abstract sense, the solar system, and the universe, are only an elastic body: chaos is an impossibility. . . .[16]

[16] *Oeuvres philosophiques*, pp. 207-208. Entropy is usually a booby-trap for non-physicists. Its applicability to Diderot's ideas of order and disorder is, to be sure, limited. Any mechanical system tends toward a state in which the unavailability of energy is at a maximum and functional organization decreases. When we assert that maximum entropy minimizes order, even though maximum stability is attained, the subjective or psychological factor intrudes into a precise, objective concept. Thus, to take an example, salt dissolved in water may be considered either as less or more orderly in comparison with salt undissolved in water. A diamond is the most highly ordered possible arrangement of carbon molecules (and the one with minimum entropy), and it is the most stable. Random carbon particles have the least order or structure or the maximum chaos but are also stable. Diderot was fully aware of the subjective factor, of the association of "order" and "disorder" with our affective and rational needs. The essential and only significant point is this: when he writes of order, what he has in mind is, precisely, organized matter and energy in highly structured form, and when he writes of stability, he is referring to such forms, not to the chaotic stability of unstructured, undifferentiated particles. Thus, both order and stability are for him counter-entropic. To disrupt such structures is therefore to increase entropy and to destroy order.

At maximum entropy there is no tendency in a system to

Diderot goes on to say that systems (universes?), if destroyed, will form again. But will they form again in the same way? Do the worlds that follow each other duplicate each other? In Diderot's fragmentary but negative answers to this question we glimpse the inseparability of chance and determinism in his thinking, and at the same time his renewed doubts about our attaining an understanding or explanation of the fundamental questions. Speaking apparently about the existing universe, he speculates, somewhat metaphysically, that nature has produced only one act (Pensée XI). Everything followed from it in a chain of cause and effect. The contrary supposition would entail incompatible collections of phenomena, and we should no longer have a "universe": "The absolute independence of a single fact is incompatible with the idea of a whole (*de tout*); and without the idea of a whole (*de tout*), philosophy is impossible."

These considerations lead us to an important point of

---

change itself. It is true that in regard to the cosmos Diderot did not conceive of entropy in this sense—at least not as a definitive state, since he believed that new worlds form from worlds dissolved. His concept is, nevertheless, entropic in two important respects. First, entropy, which is a statistical effect of probability, involves two factors: chance and very large numbers. Second, living things resist the degradation of energy and maximize its use in organized form. These are essential elements of Diderot's thought. As we shall see in the fourth chapter, one might also make a case for the role of entropy in political organizations, as he conceives of their evolution. In sum, insofar as order is for Diderot the effective organization of energy-systems, we may properly bring in the notion of entropy. The remarkable modernity of Diderot's thinking can be confirmed by a reading of the first chapter of J. Monod's *Chance and Necessity*, New York, 1972. (I am grateful to Roger Crocker for a valuable discussion on this point.)

ambiguity, on which Diderot's interpreters sometimes go astray. It is not certain whether he conceives of the universe as a Whole, in the sense of an organic unity. In order to discuss this question, which is pertinent at this place, we shall have to jump ahead to some of his later writings. In one passage in *Le Rêve de d'Alembert*, he does indeed express such a conception:

> What do you mean, with your "individuals"? There aren't any, no, none at all. There is only a single great individual, the whole. In this whole, as in a machine or in any animal, there is a part which you call such and such. But if you give the name "individual" to that part of the whole, it is only a concept as false as if, in a bird, you gave the name to the wing, to a feather of the wing.[17]

If Diderot does indeed hold this opinion, then it is contradictory to his philosophy of the emergence of levels through greater complexity, and to his important concept of organism, to which we shall shortly come. Diderot is notoriously contradictory; but in this case the contradiction may perhaps be "explained away" by the context. He is trying to establish the ideas of the chain of being, of a commonality in the three kingdoms and in all species and, even more basically, of the universality of matter and its properties ("there is no quality in which all beings do not participate"). Within such a context of ideas, an "individual" would be something outside of the world order, and a refutation of that order. There can be no "independent phenomena."[18]

[17] *Oeuvres philosophiques*, p. 312.

[18] *Oeuvres philosophiques, De l'Interprétation de la nature*, Pensée XI.

Everywhere else, Diderot denies that the universe constitutes a Whole in the sense of an organism. But he insists that it is a whole in a quite different sense. "Everything passes, *il n'y a que le tout qui reste.*"[19] If the universe were comparable to an organism, the Whole could not survive the disappearance of its constituent parts or organs. The universe is a "whole" in the sense that the causal law requires that every event have an effect, and that every effect is in turn a cause, in a linear sequence.

> Suppose a displaced molecule: the displacement was not spontaneous. The cause of its displacement has another cause, this cause another, and so on. . . . Suppose a displaced molecule: this displacement will have an effect, this effect another, and so on. . . . (*De l'Interprétation de la nature,* Pensée LVI).

This is the "essence de l'ordre," the chain in time and in space, the "wholeness" that unites in one concept the heterogeneity of matter with the homogeneity of the properties and actions of matter, and of universal process. It does not constitute an organism since the parts do not act in concord toward the realization of a single, common purpose; this can only emerge in particular configurations of matter in which a complexity of organization attains a new level that is not characteristic of the cosmos as such. The same is true of the continuity of action and reaction that is the specific mark of an organic whole. "This world is only a collection of molecules loaded in an infinity of different ways. There is a law of necessity that executes itself without design, without effort, without intelligence,

[19] *Oeuvres philosophiques,* p. 300.

without progress, without resistance, in all the works of Nature."[20]

That is why the death of worlds and the birth of new worlds will give rise to new life, but never the same forms of life. "That is because everything is connected in nature, and he who supposes a new phenomenon or brings back a past moment recreates a new world."[21] And again: "Change the whole, and you necessarily change me; but the whole is changing constantly."[22] The cosmos is in a state of constant "*fermentation*" that would be intolerable in a true organism. (In the body there is a constant turnover of materials, but it serves to maintain an identical, clearly defined and purposive structure which itself is not in such a state of turbulence.) Such a state is not only tolerable but necessary in a single system, or cosmos, where there can be no "individual" exempt from universal law and process.

To summarize: the universe is a whole insofar as it is a system of interactions. It is not unified in the way an organism is, but consists of many distinct, non-contiguous units that ultimately affect each other in certain ways (e.g., gravitation, the conditions in which living forms develop, etc.), but are independent in other ways (e.g., the death of a man on earth has no effect on a hypothetical being on Sirius, and vice versa, whereas the death of an organ would destroy the entire organism).

[20] *Salon de 1767*, in *Oeuvres complètes*, XI, p. 103. We cannot take seriously the fanciful speculation Diderot puts in the mouth of Mlle. de l'Espinasse: "Who has told you that this world does not also have its meninx, or that in some corner of space there doesn't reside a large or small spider whose threads extend everywhere?" (*Oeuvres philosophiques*, p. 316).

[21] *Oeuvres philosophiques*, p. 269.

[22] Ibid., p. 310.

Yet the world is a system, because everything is governed by the same laws and nothing is totally independent of everything else.[23] This is still enough to divide Diderot from a purely mechanical viewpoint, for which everything is dependent on a prior cause but is not required to be interdependent in the sense he implies. His universe is holistic, but not organicist. Holism, as defined in *The Oxford English Dictionary*, is "the tendency in nature to produce wholes from the ordered groupings of unit structures. . . . The real entities of the material world must, like organisms, be creative, self-transcending. . . ." Perhaps one might also say that Diderot wishes to occupy a halfway house, between Plato's "world-animal" on the one hand, and the Democritean chance-and-mechanism view on the other. However, as a materialist, he could scarcely have embraced the Platonic view (*Timaeus*) according to which the universe is a single living body in which every part is only a part of the whole. We may rather suppose that his view is closer to that of the modern physicist, that scientific statements cannot refer to individuals or individual events (inasmuch as these are unique and not strictly recurrent) outside of a system in which events are interconnected.

As Diderot reaches this stage, he realizes that the possibility of a valid "philosophy," or science, becomes more dubious. At best, our concepts and laws apply to the particular universe we know. But even within it,

[23] Diderot's speculations seem reasonably close to the modern cosmological postulate derived from the theory of relativity: "Generally speaking, the mean characteristics of the universe are the same at any point in it, at a given moment of time. . . . At least on the average, the universe is homogeneous and isotropic everywhere for any given moment" (Jean Charon, *Cosmology*, London, 1920, p. 192).

and despite the "single act," the intricate interweavings of chance and necessity produce difficulties that may well be insurmountable. "Phenomena are infinite; causes, hidden; forms, perhaps transitory" (Pensée XXII). Even the cause-effect linkage is inadequate to understanding if phenomena are transitory. "But if the state of all things is one of constant change; if nature is still at work, then, despite the chain that links phenomena, there can be no philosophy" (Pensée LVIII, para. 1). Diderot is again remarkably close to the modern view. Predictability can never be absolute because of nature's ambiguity of unique events within a fluid, changing structure of reality that enfolds and connects them. Scientific laws, which refer to reproducible situations in an ensemble of similar events, do not exclude stochastic processes. Clearly, Diderot would not disagree with the modern physicist who holds that even the fundamental constants (e.g., the speed of light) might vary with time; or that other worlds may exist (solar systems, an anti-matter universe) in which "fundamental laws" are different or even reversed. Like other materialists, he will try to "save" determinism by assuming that if all the hidden, chance variables were known, absolute causation and predictability would be guaranteed. But they can never be known, and this is one ineluctable limit to the power of science to penetrate nature's mysteries—despite his earlier assertion that he was writing to "banish mysteries," meaning religion, of course.

These reflections are a kind of background for the biological speculations. The universal law of change, the dynamism of construction, destruction, and reconstruction that impels physical events must also obtain in these more complex organizations of matter that constitute life. We are compelled to suppose "that from the beginning of time the peculiar elements of animal life were scattered and mixed in with the mass of matter; that those elements chanced to be brought together, because it was possible for that to happen" (Pensée LVIII, para. 2).

Whether or not Diderot had a concept of transformism has been debated.[24] The question should rather be to what extent he had one, and what kind of a concept it was. It was certainly not the present-day theory of organic evolution, with its tight interrelationship of mutations, adaptation to environment, and survival of the fit. Yet he does believe that life has had a history, that species evolve, and that they are interrelated. It is not clear that Diderot conceives of a species as emerging from a line of variations occurring in another, older species, or whether each is an independent *de novo* variation of a basic model. It is necessary to quote part of a well-known passage:

> Nature seems to have taken pleasure in varying a single mechanism in an infinite variety of ways. She never abandons any one kind of production until she has multiplied the individual examples to produce as many different aspects as possible. If we consider the animal kingdom and perceive that there is not a single quadruped whose functions and parts, above all the internal ones, are not entirely similar to those of another quadruped, would it not be easy to believe

[24] See, *inter alia*, L. G. Crocker, "Diderot and Eighteenth Century French Transformism," in *Forerunners of Darwin*, Baltimore, 1959, chapter V; J. Roger, *op. cit.*, p. 610 *et passim*; and review of same by L. G. Crocker, in *Romanic Review*, vol. 56 (1965), pp. 142-45.

> that in the beginning there was only one animal, a prototype of all animals, certain of whose organs nature has merely lengthened, shortened, changed, multiplied, or obliterated? Imagine the fingers of your hand joined together and the material of which the nails are made becoming suddenly so abundant that they spread and swell, enveloping and covering the whole extremity: instead of a hand you have a horse's hoof. When we see the successive metamorphoses of the prototype's outward appearance, whatever it may have been in the first place, bring one kingdom gradually and imperceptibly nearer to another kingdom, and people the boundaries of those two kingdoms (if one may use the term "boundaries" where there is no real division), and people, I repeat, the boundaries of those two kingdoms with uncertain, ambiguous beings, stripped to a great degree of the forms, the qualities and the functions of the one and taking on the forms, qualities, and the functions of the other, is it not difficult to resist the belief that there was never more than one first being, a prototype of all other beings? (Pensée XII).

In a later passage Diderot comes closer to affirming that species arise one from another, or at least from the original living form. A species is defined as a kind of order.

> Who will prevent elementary, intelligent and sensitive parts from straying infinitely from the order that constitutes the species? It follows from this that an infinity of animal species may have come out of a first animal; an infinity of beings from a first being; all nature, a single act (Pensée L).

He is entertaining an unquestionably transformist notion (though not our theory), when he reports in a letter about a discussion with d'Holbach:

> I pointed out suns in the sky that were beginning to light up and others that were dying out. . . . I added: ours, then, can therefore undergo the same fate. Tell me then what becomes of the whole animal kingdom? It disappears. But if I rekindle the sun, I see plants, fruits, insects, and in all likelihood animals and men, natural productions of the soil, reborn. [Up to this point the idea is not transformist.] —And man? you will ask me. —Yes: man, but not as he is. First, a certain something; then another certain something; and then, after several hundreds of millions of years and so many more certain somethings, the bipedal animal who has the name of man.[25]

And he adds: "Just as in the animal and vegetable kingdoms an individual begins, so to speak, grows, lasts, decays and passes away; is it not the same with entire species?" (Pensée LVIII, para. 2).

We must suppose that the original "embryo" has traversed "an infinite number of structurings and developments." These are characterized by increasing complexity. With each level of complexity, new potentials gradually emerge—movement, sensation, thought, self-consciousness, emotions, language, and all the attributes of culture. Time brings all about, and nothing can be understood atemporally. He urges the reader to recognize "why I have introduced the notions of past, present and future into some of my propositions; and

[25] "A Madame de Maux (?), été de 1769 (?)," in Diderot, *Correspondance*, ed. Georges Roth, Paris, 1963, vol. IX, 95-96.

why I have inserted the idea of sequence [becoming] into my definition of nature" (Pensée LVIII). Millions of years go by between each development. Each development reaches a platform of stability. Then disorder gradually invades it. Death, dispersion and a new re-ordering ensue.[26]

Evolution does involve a chain of beings, and Diderot clearly states this hypothesis:

> The chain of beings is not broken by the diversity of forms. The form is often only a deceptive mask, and the link that seems to be missing exists perhaps in a known being, to which the progress of comparative anatomy has not yet been able to assign its true place.[27]

While Diderot's idea may have an ultimate Leibnizian origin, it is expressed here in terms of biological progression and the interrelation of species.

How matter organizes itself into living forms is a question that perplexes Diderot in all his writings on the subject. Does inorganic matter become life by restructuring itself to produce "sensitivity"? Or does "sensitivity" exist in latent or degraded form in non-living substances, awaiting activation by some process such as chemical fermentation (spontaneous generation) or ingestion? He is never able to decide between the two alternatives, or indeed to believe for long, with any real conviction, in either one.[28] We need not go into

[26] See also *Eléments de physiologie*, édition critique par Jean Mayer, Paris, 1964, pp. 42, 51. All references to this work will be to this edition.

[27] Ibid., p. 6.

[28] In later years, he called the notion of universal sensitivity a convenient notion, and no more (*Réfutation d'Helvétius*, in *Oeuvres philosophiques*, pp. 565-68).

the details of his discussions of these possibilities, since they concern the mode of effectuation of a principle that both exemplify equally: the reaching outward and "upward" toward new complexities of structure possessing viability; that is, stability of the power to resist deterioration to a lower level of structuring and degradation of energy.

In *De l'Interprétation de la nature,* Diderot prefers the hypothesis of an omnipresent "sensibilité sourde" which was activated at a certain point of time when circumstances favored the proper structuring that produced the leap to a new level of emergence (Pensée LI). Diderot's basic law of nature, though not adequate to account clearly or fully for such a prodigy, is still the explanation, and he gives it a lucid if somewhat poetic formulation:

> As a result of this muted sensitivity and of the varying configurations of all organic molecules, it would then be clear that there could be only one situation in nature for which each of them was properly fitted. Each molecule would therefore have been impelled, by an automatic and constant feeling of discomfort, to seek out the situation proper to it, just as we see animals move about in their sleep, when the use of almost all their faculties is in abeyance, until they have found the position most suited for repose. The use of this principle, with no further help, would have embraced, quite simply and without any dangerous implications, all the phenomena he [Maupertuis] was undertaking to explain, as well as all those numberless marvels that keep our observers of insects in such a perpetual state of amazement; and it would have provided him with the following general definition of an animal: *a system of different organic mole-*

cules that have combined with one another, under the impulsion of a sensation similar to an obtuse and muffled sense of touch given to them by the creator of matter as a whole, until each one of them has found the most suitable position for its shape and comfort.[29]

Diderot is aware of the inadequacy of his conceptualization. He brings it out in his distinction between the observer and the interpreter of nature. The latter goes beyond evidence to conjecture, but cautiously: "he rises to the very essence of order; he sees that the *pure and simple* coexistence of a sensitive and thinking being with some chain or other of causes and effects does not suffice for him to make an absolute judgment; he stops there; if he took another step, he would be going outside of nature" (Pensée LVI).

It is also important to note that the workings of basic law are apparently mechanical, even though the emergents may go beyond mechanism to new kinds of interrelationships, with their own qualities and laws. The metaphor of "a comfortable situation" and the word "arrangement" are indicative only of motion and position, and of stability of structure. On the other hand, the vague notion of muted or latent sensitivity ("sensibilité inerte" or "sensibilité sourde"), which Diderot frequently though tentatively attributes to all matter as an inherent property, leaves the interpreter of Diderot in a situation of uncertainty that the *philosophe* does not alleviate by his own doubts about such a supposition. Its appeal is frankly in its convenience, for Diderot knows that he cannot really conceive of the appearance of life on purely mechanical grounds: "the impossibility of explaining the formation of a plant or an animal by

[29] Ibid., p. 231.

attraction, inertia, mobility, impenetrability, movement, matter or extension has led the philosopher Baumann [Maupertuis] to posit still other properties in nature" (Pensée L).

In 1769 Diderot composed his major statement of a materialist philosophy. The trilogy called *Le Rêve de d'Alembert,* which was not published until 1830, covers wide ground, including psychology, sexuality, and morals. In this unitary vision, all else stems from the fundamental metaphysical position and, as in *De l'Interprétation de la nature,* from its biological extensions; but biological questions are even more in the forefront.

The two are indeed quite inseparable in Diderot's mind. After commencing with a restatement of the ideas that potential energy can become kinetic energy, that motion is omnipresent in immobile bodies, and that "inert sensitivity" can become active by ingestion, he expounds a theory of biological dynamics:

> The imperceptible worm wriggling in the mud is perhaps moving toward the state of a large animal. The enormous animal that frightens us by his size, is perhaps moving toward the worm's state and may be only a peculiar and momentary production of this planet.

The process of biological structuring is a particular but necessary configuration of the general world-process. When catastrophe or maximum entropy does its work, matter, hence motion remain, and all must begin again:

> When the sun is extinguished, what will happen then? The plants will perish, the animals will perish, and the earth remains solitary and still. Light up that star again, and immediately you renew the necessary cause of an infinite number of new productions. I

> would not dare to say whether our present-day plants and animals would or would not reappear, among them, after centuries have gone by.[30]

The same propulsive forces which constitute the very nature of matter (and there is nothing but matter) create a chaotic universe in which all order is transient, though at any given moment real:

> The world begins and ends constantly. At every moment it is at its beginning and at its end. It has never had any other, and will never have any other.[31] In this immense ocean of matter, not one molecule is identical with itself for a single instant. *Rerum novus nascitur ordo* ["a new order of things is born"]—that is its eternal inscription.[32]

These statements are refinements on earlier ones. The most important step forward in the *Rêve de d'Alembert* is the conceptualization of the notion of organism, which involves the emergence of novelty.[33] Beyond a certain level of complexity, a structuration comes about that creates a new type of interrelationships, an enhancement of organized energy to the point of a new way of existing.

[30] Ibid., p. 268.

[31] A steady-state, rather than a "big-bang" concept seems to be implied now.

[32] Ibid., p. 300.

[33] For earlier studies of the idea of organism in Diderot, see M. Wartofsky, *op. cit.*, and especially Ian Alexander, "Philosophy of Organism and Philosophy of Consciousness in Diderot's speculative Thought," in *Studies in Romance Philology and French Literature presented to John Orr*, Manchester, 1953, pp. 1-21. Alexander, however, takes liberties that go far beyond what is justified by the texts.

Diderot reaches this concept through the realization that a living body is a whole, or a unity, that is not explicable by the simple idea of an aggregate, or the addition of new parts. "But how was this unity brought about?" asks Mlle. de l'Espinasse in the dialogue. "Look, philosopher: I do see an aggregate, a tissue of tiny sensitive beings; but an animal . . . a whole, a single system, *it*, with the consciousness of its unity!"[34] Diderot allows her to supply her own answer. As contiguity becomes continuity, there is set up "habitual action and reaction" (the phrase is stated twice). "Everything then works together to produce a kind of unity, that exists only in the animal."[35] In other words, what has emerged is a Whole, which is more than and different from the mere sum of its parts. "All our organs . . . are only distinct animals that the law of continuity binds into a sympathy, a unity, an all-embracing identity."[36]

In the *Eléments de physiologie*, Diderot's last *summa* (completed in its present form in 1784), the concept will be further developed. "A general, common sensitivity is established, which the organs share in different ways."[37] The Whole possesses its own reality, its own properties, different from those of its parts. The new system of interactions is governed by the Whole, thus displacing the operative principle from external causality, or force, to internal impulsion. The behavior of the system is unpredictable from that of its separate parts or the subassemblies of its parts. "There are certainly two distinct kinds of life, even three. The life of the whole animal. The life of each of its organs. The life of the

[34] *Oeuvres philosophiques*, p. 288.

[35] Ibid., p. 290.

[36] Ibid., p. 293.

[37] *Eléments de physiologie*, p. 26.

molecule."[38] "The animal is a unitary whole (*un tout un*), and it is perhaps that unity that constitutes the soul, the self, and consciousness, with the help of memory."[39] In other words, the animal exists and functions simultaneously on three levels of structure and law, but the highest level dominates:

> The organ is an object subject to comfort and discomfort, to comfort that it seeks and discomfort from which it strives to free itself. . . . Difference between the whole and the organ: the whole looks ahead, and the organ does not. The whole experiments, the organ does not. The whole avoids harm; the organ does not avoid it, but feels it and tries to free itself from it.[40]

Organs can, however, acquire needs and habits which may impose themselves on the whole animal and give us our vices and our virtues.[41] The body is a machine in which everything is interconnected and reciprocating.

Each organ, then, has its own life and its own demands; yet it exists not for itself, but for the whole organism it obeys. It is obvious from the last few quotations that the organism is characterized by purposiveness. Its purpose is to preserve its being; that is, to protect its complex ordering from the invasion of disorder that, according to the basic law, is its inevitable fate. "What is a plant? What is an animal? a coordination of infinitely active molecules, a chain of small forces which everything works to break up. It is not surprising, then, that these beings disappear so quickly."[42]

In lower animals, the purpose of the organism is accomplished by instinct, which compels it to execute "a

[38] Ibid., p. 27. See pp. 283 ff. for a detailed statement.

[39] Ibid., p. 59.

[40] Ibid., p. 266.

[41] Ibid., pp. 287, 293, 295.

[42] Ibid., p. 8.

long sequence of operations proper for its self-preservation."[43] In higher animals, and especially in man, the brain or *sensorium commune* is the directing control center to which all organs report and by which they are regulated. As Bordeu says in the *Rêve*: "Therefore there is something in you that knows whether it is your hand or your thigh that has been stung, and that thing is not your foot or even your hand that has been stung; your hand suffers, but something else knows it, and it does not suffer."[44] The brain is the center, like the spider in its web, receiving and correlating the sensory input from the outside world and from the organs of the inner world of the organism itself. "In the center it is informed of what is going on in any spot of the apartment it has hung."[45] It also determines the reaction, or output, which Diderot calls judgment: "Yes, there are the five witnesses; but the judge or the recorder? There is one particular organ, the brain, to which the five witnesses make the report."[46] This "controller" has no other function.

> Disturb the center of the nervous system, and you change the animal. It seems that there is where he is, completely, at times dominating the branches, at times dominated by them.
>
> And the animal is in a state of despotism or of anarchy.[47]

The specific property of the brain is to collect and to remember information; the brain is a "memory bank."[48]

[43] Ibid., p. 32. [44] *Oeuvres philosophiques*, p. 307.

[45] Ibid., p. 315.

[46] *Réfutation d'Helvétius*, in *Oeuvres complètes*, vol. II, p. 318.

[47] *Le Rêve de d'Alembert*, in *Oeuvres philosophiques*, p. 346; also, pp. 330-31, 256-57.

[48] Ibid., pp. 353-54.

It is memory that creates a "self" in man, the feeling of identity over time.[49] There is a precise statement in the *Réfutation d'Helvétius*:

> . . . without a unifier and a common judge of all sensations, without an organ to remember all that happens to us, each sense, a sensitive and living instrument, might have a fleeting consciousness of its existence, but there would certainly be no consciousness of the whole animal or man.[50]

In man and in man alone self-awareness creates a self-transcendence. "The distinctive characteristic of man is his brain, not his external structure."[51] He is only a harpsichord of a complex sort, Diderot says; but, "he is at the same time the musician and the instrument."[52] Elsewhere he puts it this way: man is both the book and the reader.[53] Sensitivity plus memory allow this.

Scientific thought was entering a junction that bifurcated into a particulate and an organismic theory. Boyle, for instance, opposed any view of nature as organism or force (nature with a majuscule), because it would put a force between God and man and make God superfluous, and also because the particulate approach lent itself to experiment and to mathematical treatment. The French materialists affirmed that nature unfolded itself. Diderot's universe was also particulate, but within the

[49] Ibid., pp. 341-43; *Eléments de physiologie*: "La mémoire constitue le soi" (p. 244). See Jean Perkins, *The Concept of the Self in the French Enlightenment*, Genève, 1969, chapter V, for an excellent analysis.

[50] *Oeuvres philosophiques*, p. 585.

[51] *Eléments de physiologie*, p. 48.

[52] *Le Rêve de d'Alembert*, in *Oeuvres philosophiques*, pp. 273-74.

[53] *Eléments de physiologie*, p. 243.

framework of a self-creating cosmos. On the biological level, he considered the organism or Whole, and not the particles or parts, to be the significant and the directing force. Modern biology has taken the opposite path, and its great triumphs have sprung from the particulate approach. Its materialism is quite different from that of La Mettrie, Diderot, or d'Holbach. Organismic activity is too vague and hard to deal with. It is only very recently that some biologists, such as Dobzhansky and Dubos, in full awareness of the triumphs of particulate biology, have begun to place renewed emphasis on organism as a level and a reality of its own, whose peculiar activity cannot be ignored. (Their forerunners were Driesch and the vitalist school around 1900, and the various "emergent" theories that flourished in the 1920's, but they are not strictly comparable.) At a further remove, but no less important and even more basic, is the conclusion of modern physics, as formulated by J. M. Jauch: "The behavior of quantal systems furnishes us with new points of view concerning the essential properties of composite systems, where it is recognized that the sum of the parts does not at all exhaust the properties of the whole" (*op. cit.*, p. 96).

One question on which scholars differ—to what degree Diderot escapes from mechanism and to what degree he remains a mechanist—is ultimately fruitless, because it is undecidable.[54] The vagueness of his ideas

[54] Thus J. Roger writes: "The deepest source of Diderot's thought and his vision of the world is still and always the philosophy of Epicurus and Lucretius. . . . Needham allowed Diderot to rejuvenate Spinoza; he did not suggest a new vision of the world to him" (*op. cit.*, p. 664). Most recent commentators would take a contrary view. Cf. Ian Alexander and Jean Varloot, *op. cit.* According to Colm Kiernan, "it was Diderot's aim to destroy the

and of his vocabulary allows considerable latitude and makes it well nigh impossible for a reader, two centuries later, to find his way back into the intellectual context with real precision.[55]

Diderot surely discarded the simple mechanism of Lucretius and the seventeenth-century iatrophysicists. In the 1740's it was obvious to some thinkers that the phenomena of life were too complex to be accounted for in that way. Qualitative differences or novelties accompany new combinations of matter, which are not mere aggregations but the establishment of new kinds of relationships with their own laws. The difficulty begins when we reach the organic level. In such advanced structures, does matter obey laws other than those of mechanics? But we do not even know what words such as "mechanical" and "machine" include or denote for Diderot. The foetus grows "by eating and by other purely mechanical operations," by heat and movement.[56] "With one inert matter, structured in a certain way, impregnated by another inert matter, we get sensitivity,

---

mechanical world-view" (*op. cit.*, p. 137). This statement seems to be acceptable only insofar as some had considered the world to be a static machine, rather than an evolving one—unique, of course, since there can be no other like it.

[55] According to twentieth-century physics, new qualities are predictable, but non-mechanically. "Non-mechanical" usually refers to quantum mechanics, in which some predictability can be achieved at the expense of other aspects of reality (either location in space-time, or motion, but not both). Discontinuous degrees and states of motions (energy or vibration) cause the qualitative differences in the elements, so that one might figuratively speak of "qualities" as inhering in energy or motion—an idea that Diderot approaches.

[56] *Le Rêve de d'Alembert, Oeuvres philosophiques*, p. 265, also, p. 275.

life, memory, conscience, passions, thought."[57] "Monsters" result from genetic errors, which are purely mechanical errors.[58] Men are described as "instruments endowed with sensitivity and memory," and as a specially organized harpsichord. He frequently calls men and animals machines: "a machine as complex as an animal."[59] "He is a thinking-machine (*une machine à réflexion*)," a machine designed to think.[60] In the *Entretien d'un philosophe avec la Maréchale* (1774), animals are described as machines, and man as "an animal somewhat more perfected than others."[61]

There are different kinds of machines. Animals, as Diderot says, are a special kind of machine, and man is even more special. It is preferable, I think, not to try to explain his thinking by a reduction to Leibnizianism with some novel variations, as Ian Alexander has done. No doubt the influence of Leibniz was strong, especially the ideas of the monad as a center of force, the law of continuity, the chain of being. Maupertuis, La Mettrie, Voltaire, and others were also greatly influenced by Leibniz. But Diderot's thought is unique in his time. Its uniqueness is not best accounted for in metaphysical terms, such as characterize Leibniz, nor as the union of the subjective and objective, of heterogeneity and homogeneity, of idealism and realism, although such interpretations are logically inferable. Diderot often had the genius to "smell out" (to use his own word) ideas that were to make their fortune in the future. His conception of the animal, and of man, as machines, is justifiable in twentieth-century terms. We are indeed

[57] Ibid., p. 276.
[58] Ibid., pp. 325, 266.
[59] Ibid., p. 325.
[60] *Réfutation d'Helvétius* in *Oeuvres complètes*, II, p. 568.
[61] *Oeuvres philosophiques*, p. 544.

cybernetic machines, self-regulating feed-back mechanisms. While Diderot could not have had a clear notion of such a machine, if we look back on what has been said of his philosophy of organicism, of the role of the brain and its relation to other organs, it is quite clear that he had more than the germ of such a concept.

"The animal body is a system of actions and reactions," he says in the *Eléments de physiologie*.[62] This is true of all living organisms, as we have seen. In higher animals, a level of consciousness is reached, and this is one major difference (but not the only difference) between a "machine de chair" and a "machine de fer" (a machine of flesh and a machine of iron).[63] In man alone, consciousness becomes self-consciousness, which is a new level or mode of being in the world. "I feel, I think, I judge; therefore a portion of organized matter, such as I, can feel, think and judge."[64] In sum, while the functioning of the elements composing the organism may be in accord with the usual laws of matter, the result is not comparable to machines made by man.

This broad conceptualization leads to difficulties in the human instance. Self-awareness surely implies a kind of freedom or self-determination not existing at the lower levels. It creates the possibility of genuine choice. This Diderot cannot and does not allow, in the *Rêve* or elsewhere: there can be no exception to universal law.[65] But within this law, which allows and

[62] Ibid., p. 61. [63] Ibid., p. 35.

[64] *Réfutation d'Helvétius* in *Oeuvres complètes*, II, p. 564.

[65] Some scholars, like Grava, attempt to argue that Diderot believed in "moral freedom," but never quote specific texts. The texts say the contrary, that freedom is an illusion, or the consciousness of a necessary choice. "The will is no less mechanical than the understanding. . . . Nothing goes by jumps in nature. Everything is linked. The animal, man, everything is subject to this

fosters the appearance of levels, man is unique; and so he vigorously refutes the reductionism of Helvétius' *De l'Homme*. Judgment is not reducible to sensation: "That is a far-fetched conclusion; it is more suited to animality in general than to men. . . . I am a man, and I must have causes particular to man."[66] What, precisely, is signified by the last phrase? Nothing less than the emergence of a whole new way of being in the world. Not only reflection and judgment, but culture: social conditioning, a moral heritage, education.

But there is something more important yet. The basic law has acquired a new mode of operation in a still different way. For the first time the primacy of the individual emerges, despite Diderot's insistence that from the viewpoint of determinism or the universal cause-effect law there are no "individuals." At the in-

general law" (*Eléments de physiologie*, p. 262. See, among other statements, the firm conviction in *Jacques le Fataliste, Oeuvres romanesques*, pp. 498, 670-71, 757-58). It would be more accurate and fruitful to say that what Diderot stipulates is new kinds of necessary causes, peculiar to man. "Free will" would be the end of whatever order there is; it would be the sign of universal disorder.

However, the bit of nonsense in *Jacques le Fataliste* (p. 513) implies the possibility of contradictory truths, and leads to this: "And what did they do there? Jacques said, What was written up there; his master, what he willed: and they were both right." In modern terms, the question is logically meaningless. It is neither an analytic statement, capable of being falsified by the law of contradiction, nor a synthetic statement, capable of empirical verification or falsification. Diderot seems to intuit this position, playfully.

[66] *Oeuvres philosophiques*, p. 564. Alexander comments that a being having the power of choice and selection from external data (the input) is both a value and the initiator of value (*op. cit.*, p. 6).

organic level, each molecule seeks its "most comfortable position," thus initiating structure. At the organic level, the search for "pleasure" and the avoidance of pain is the analogous expression of the *conatus* to persist against change and increasing entropy. This, too, is universal, and includes man.[67] At that level, however, the species gives the law to the individual. With man, this is no longer so: "Physical sensitivity is about the same in all of us, and yet each of us has his own kind of happiness."[68] The reason for this is that at the level of complexity that characterizes the human structure, especially the brain, the peculiar "organization" or heredity of each individual is the most significant factor:

> I agree that man combines ideas, just as a fish swims and a bird flies; but each man is swept along by his structure, his character, his temperament, his natural aptitude for preferably combining one kind of ideas rather than other kinds.[69]

Each brain, each mind is different. It is wrong, Diderot insists, to take "the conditions of all animal action, in general, for the motive of the act of an individual of a species of animal called man."[70]

With individuality, the reality of the self also emerges. The self is the realm of self-conscious subjectivity, actualized in a continually changing being by memory.[71] The work of the mind in a special sense reproduces the universal law: it constitutes order out of the chaos of sensations. This order corresponds to the objective order

[67] *Oeuvres philosophiques*, p. 567.

[68] *Réfutation d'Helvétius* in *Oeuvres complètes*, II, 318.

[69] *Oeuvres philosophiques*, p. 570.

[70] Ibid., p. 567.

[71] See Jean A. Perkins, *op. cit.*, p. 122 *et passim.*

of relationships in nature ("This *liaison* is necessary"[72]); but the orderly assemblage is also a human and an individual one. Diderot makes this quite clear. Much is rejected or stored in the unconscious memory; the rest is organized into patterns and stored where it is subject to recall.[73]

In this way and in this measure, we may speak of self-consciousness being its own cause, and of subjectivity, of energy consciously directed.[74] Goal-directed action, or behavior, is common to all animals. In man it is, to an important extent, conscious and willed. That is why he exists on a moral level of pleasure and pain that is quite distinct from the physical, and why he uniquely can have non-egoistic motives.[75]

The highest level in individuality is the genius, who

[72] *Eléments de physiologie*, pp. 233-34.

[73] The pertinent passages are all noted in Perkins, p. 125. Mrs. Perkins concludes "It is, therefore, an actual physical entity which gives unity to the varied sensations and emotions which assail a man during his lifetime, and this organ has a directing energy of its own which permits it to shape the various elements which the outer, and the inner world offers to it. The way in which experience is organized depends upon the original structure of this particular organ, and also upon the way in which it has assimilated previous experiences."

[74] Alexander, *op. cit.*, pp. 6, 19. Alexander, however, goes well beyond Diderot's own thought when he asserts that the human consciousness grasps the image of eternity, of "one single Being accomplishing one single act in an eternal present where past, present and future are merged" (p. 17). Not only is this conclusion not implied in Diderot's texts, but it is precisely because man does not have that view that science is "impossible." We similarly cannot accept Alexander's claim that for Diderot the consciousness mirrors and comprehends the world in its infinity (p. 13). This is Leibniz. Diderot always said that we are unable to do that.

[75] *Réfutation d'Helvétius* in *Oeuvres complètes*, II, pp. 566-67, 573-74.

represents a kind of uniqueness within human uniqueness. He may be a law unto himself, and Diderot sometimes discusses (notably in the *Entretien d'un père avec ses enfants*) the validity of his putting himself above the law. But in *Le Neveu de Rameau*, the interlocutor, "Moi," tries to reconcile the genius with the good of the species.[76] Jean Fabre has remarked that "the demands of individualism and the primacy of the species" are fully reconciled only in the genius; a society's worth "is measured by its ability to integrate superior men, even when they seem to enter into conflict with it."[77] To this penetrating remark we must, however, add another consideration. In Diderot's own pre-Nietzschean view of the genius, the reconciliation does not take place during the latter's lifetime. The present is in a sense sacrificed to the future. The genius is a disorderly element, but the disorder may be the promise of a better order, through his contribution. The working of history, depending heavily on the factor of great men, has a character analogous to that of natural process—an interplay of the chaotic and the orderly.

Materialism, Diderot has come to realize, is a useful philosophy, the only possible philosophy for investigation of the material world. It is disastrous when applied *tel quel* to the inner, subjective world of human thought and emotion. When materialism is used to deny the reality of human experience and to dehumanize man, it has overstepped its bounds. Man's place in nature, his humanity, are defined not by his animality, Diderot proclaims, but by his humanity.

[76] *Le Neveu de Rameau*, édition critique par Jean Fabre, Genève et Lille, 1950, p. 14. All references to *Le Neveu de Rameau* will be to this edition.

[77] Ibid., p. 140.

The moral problem springs from this peculiar situation. In the first place, men (as Rousseau had shown) are not social animals in a natural way, acting necessarily for the group or species. As a self-directing individual, man, at least in advanced civilizations, is at odds with the directives of his society: this is the theme of the *Supplément au Voyage de Bougainville,* among other writings of Diderot. There is no simple way to account for human behavior. We see this in Diderot's literary practice more than in his philosophical reflection. "Rameau is at one and the same time what he is by his nature, what his environment has made him, and what he has made himself and is making himself every day by his behavior."[78] In the second place, the universal law requiring the search for pleasure (with man, we may properly speak of happiness), combined with the primacy of individual "organization" ("each man is swept away by his structure, his character, his temperament"), makes morality impossible, except as a social imposition or tyranny. "There is only one passion, that of being happy. . . . It is vice or virtue according to its violence, its means and its effects."[79] Diderot sees the gap between abstract morality and individual need. From both the cosmic and the individual viewpoints, Bordeu concludes: "There is nothing solid except drinking, eating, living, loving and sleeping."[80] (Rameau's nephew also maintains this viewpoint against his moralistic challenger.) Vice and virtue, declares Bordeu, must be transformed into "bienfaisance" and "malfaisance." "We are *heureusement* or *malheureusement nés.* Without

[78] Guy Besse, "Observations sur la *Réfutation d'Helvétius* de Diderot," *Diderot Studies VI,* p. 39.

[79] *Eléments de physiologie,* p. 266.

[80] *Le Rêve de d'Alembert,* p. 300.

being aware of it, we are swept away by an overwhelming torrent that leads some to glory and others to ignominy."[81] The relativity is undeniable. So is the absence of any foundation for a moral order in the cosmos:

> The fact is that there is neither absolute good or evil in the whole; the fact is that it is an absurdity to suppose in the whole a mélange of good or bad laws, in order to deduce from it the good or evil of individuals. "Good" and "evil" can no more be said of the universe than of a particular machine in which there is one part that wears down another. . . . At any moment we can say of the universe that everything in it is just the way it is absolutely necessary for it to be. Nothing to blame, nothing to praise.[82]

Morality is a new level of existence, which emerges with man and belongs to him. The implicit contradiction is not in Diderot, but in man, who is both determined and self-directing, both a physical and a moral being. It turns out that the acme of the cosmic ordering process is a creature who is an element of disorder, by his nature. This is indeed cosmic irony.

Diderot was convinced, even to the point of silly fantasy,[83] of the tendency of all matter to organize itself in ever more complex structures.

> If the perhaps infinite sum of the possibly infinite multitude of nature's molecules were completely known to us, it seems evident to me that we should see all phenomena occurring according to rigorously

[81] Ibid., p. 364. [82] *Eléments de physiologie*, pp. 329-330.
[83] Ibid., p. 341.

geometrical laws, to which the principle of conservation, or rather the ordering, regulating principle of the universe, would be rigorously subjected. For what does it matter if there is or is not any perfectly regular body, or none perfectly consistent? Actions and reactions, whatever their number and their energy, are nonetheless geometrical; the contrary assertion is not carefully enough thought out, not philosophical enough.[84]

Life emerges at the proper point.[85] The same principle of seeking stability, or persistence in the acquired structure, obtains at all levels, and is expressed metaphorically as an idea of comfort. At the level of subjectivity, we are most acutely aware of this principle during illness, when the sick organ and the "whole machine" struggle against destructive forces.[86]

The opposite force, or increasing entropy, is also clearly formulated: "Who knows whether everything is not moving toward a reduction to a great inert, immobile sediment? Who knows what the duration of that inertia will be? Who knows what new race may emerge yet again from such a vast mass of sensitive and living points?"[87] Every structure deteriorates with time: "The general order of nature changes ceaselessly. In the midst of this mutability can a species go on the same? No; only the molecule is eternal and inalterable."[88]

[84] Ibid., p. 330.

[85] Ibid., p. 40.

[86] "Nature at all times acts in the sick man as the discomfort of the machine acts during sleep; it moves spontaneously, stirs about until it has found the most comfortable situation. . . ." (Ibid., p. 300.)

[87] *Le Rêve de d'Alembert*, p. 302.

[88] *Eléments de physiologie*, p. 42.

It would be improper to speak, as some Marxists have done, of Diderot's thought as being an early form of dialectic. There is no unity of contraries producing a new synthesis. Construction derives from the addition of variegated particles, which are not contraries. There is a conflict of contraries only in the basic law itself, of increasing and decreasing entropy—antitheses which undo each other endlessly in their eternal conflict. Emergence and dialectic are not equivalents.

It is not illegitimate to infer (though Diderot never says so explicitly) that the highest organizations of matter are precisely the most subject to perturbations.

> Can you easily persuade yourself that in a machine like man, in which everything is so tightly intermeshed, in which all the organs act and react on each other, one of the parts, solid or fluid, can be diseased without affecting the others adversely? . . . You will not deny, then, that almost no man is born without some of those defects in his organization, or that time, diet, exercise, suffering and pleasures delay long in introducing them into us. . . .[89]

That is why a living structure is short-lived compared to inorganic forms. Even shorter-lived are the "monsters"—nature's mistakes. "Man is only a common production, the monster a rare one. Both are equally natural, equally necessary, equally within the general and universal order."[90] These "mistakes" become increasingly frequent with the increasing complexity of organization, according to the law of probability. "There is only one way of being healthy, an infinite number of ways of being sick."[91] The disturbance may

[89] *Réfutation d'Helvétius*, pp. 612-13.

[90] Ibid., pp. 310-11.

[91] *Eléments de physiologie*, p. 296.

come from an external invasion "which introduces disorder," or from an internal dysfunction. Other abnormalities are hereditary or foetal. A slight change in the position or in the number of the foetal "threads" suffices to make a monster.[92] The principle of disorder is within man.[93]

Taking the broadest possible point of view in one of his poetic speculations, Diderot suggests that all life is a "monstrosity," in the sense that living things are "sports" of nature that are inherently unstable forms of ordering: "Why shouldn't we consider man, why shouldn't we consider all animals as kinds of monsters that live a little longer? . . . The universe sometimes seems only a collection of monstrous beings."[94]

Such a conception tends to visualize order and disorder as objective components of cosmic process. They are the real manifestations of the laws of that process, laws that represent the capacity of matter to organize itself. However, Diderot is constantly aware that more often than not we use the terms *order* and *disorder* to express subjective reactions to phenomena. In an objective examination of nature, it is even difficult sometimes to discern one from the other:

> All the internal viscera, from the beginning of the aesophagus to the end of the intestinal canal, the lungs, heart, stomach, spleen, can be in an order that is the reverse of the common order, which we call "the natural order," without any harmful result for the system.[95]

[92] *Le Rêve de d'Alembert*, p. 325.

[93] *Eléments de physiologie*, p. 322.

[94] Ibid., pp. 208-209.

[95] Ibid., pp. 209-10. J. Roger has pointed out similarities to Buffon's outlook. See "Diderot et Buffon en 1749," in *Diderot*

Men, faced with a world that their intelligence compels them to objectify, are never free of their own subjectivity. The psyche is so constituted that at any given moment it perceives or experiences (as Diderot had shown in the *Lettre sur les aveugles*) an order of things; only the human awareness of the dimension of time enables us to transcend the appearance. This leads the philosopher to distrust judgments concerning order and disorder, as Diderot makes clear in an important passage of which we have already quoted the first few lines:

> Abbé, let's make the application. This world is only a mass of molecules loaded in an infinity of different ways. There is a law of necessity that operates without design, without effort, without intelligence, without progress, without resistance in all of Nature's works. . . . This beautiful order that enchants you in the universe cannot be other than what it is. You know only one, the one you live in. You find it alternatively beautiful or ugly, according to whether you coexist with it in a pleasant or painful way. If it were a quite different order, it would be equally beautiful or ugly for those who would coexist with it in a pleasant or painful way. An inhabitant of Saturn, transported to earth, would feel his lungs torn to pieces, and would perish, cursing nature. An inhabitant of the earth, transported to Saturn, would feel stifled, suffocated, and would perish, cursing nature. . . .
>
> My dear abbé, I said to him, forget for a moment

Studies IV, p. 232, especially the idea that the "perpetual play of destruction and renewal" is an order, but one that for us is really a disorder. Roger recalls Diderot's more or less sincere letter to Voltaire (11 juin 1749) in which he says of atheists, "I have noticed that the charms of order captivate them in spite of themselves" (p. 236).

the grain of sand that is irritating your cornea and listen to me. Why does the universe seem an order to you? It is because everything is linked, in its place, and because there is not a single being that does not have a sufficient reason, unknown or known, for his position, his production, his effect. Can the west wind be an exception? Can grains of sand be an exception? Can windstorms? If all the forces animating each of the molecules that formed the wind which has enveloped us were known, a geometrician would prove to you that the one that inserted itself between your eye and eyelid is exactly in its place.

But, said the abbé, I'd rather have it somewhere else. I am in pain, and the landscape we have left was most pleasant to my sight.

And what does nature care about that! Did she arrange the landscape for you?

Why not?

Because if she has ordered the landscape for you, then she has also ordered the windstorm for you. Come now, my friend, let's not count ourselves so important. We are in nature; we are sometimes comfortable, sometimes uncomfortable. Believe me, those who praise nature for carpeting the earth in springtime with green, a friendly color to the eye, are impertinent fellows who are forgetting that this nature, whose beneficence they insist on finding everywhere and in everything, spreads over our countryside in winter a vast white blanket that hurts our eyes, makes us turn our heads away, and exposes us to death by freezing. Nature is good and beautiful when it favors us; she is ugly and evil when she afflicts us. Often she owes a great part of her charms to our own efforts.[96]

[96] *Salon de 1767*, in *Oeuvres complètes*, vol. XI, pp. 103-104, 108-109.

These passages contain intimations of man's alienation in a meaningless universe. In *Jacques le Fataliste*, the hero's motto, "It was written up there," is in itself indicative of a directing force, though whether its nature is that of a plan or of utter caprice is unknowable. This suprahuman reality is not meaningful in human terms. It strikes us in any case as a disorder, whatever it may be. Jacques' motto thus has a high symbolic value. "Direction," or law, and disorder are coexistent contraries. The universe is matter and process. While we cannot understand matter, process is apprehended in terms of order and disorder, of structuring and disintegration. But it is not only the "content" of the process that is so apprehended—this is our human view on what results, on what exists. The mode of operation of the process strikes us equally, intellectually and affectively, as a tension between these contraries.

Diderot, however, unlike Voltaire, does not capitalize on these possibilities. He notes them as part of the human condition, as our existential truth, and rejects anthropocentrism. He looks at man as part of the cosmic order, much more than he considers the latter in relation to man. As he contemplates the cosmic process in its full and vast scope, he realizes that the question of order and disorder is one without an answer, even without a meaning. Everything is built and everything is destroyed. Everything changes, and in some way everything is reborn. It is all chance, and it is all necessity. Diderot is perhaps alone, in his century, in his recognition of the coexistence of contrary truths—today an accepted scientific principle. In *Jacques le Fataliste* he shows, more vividly than in any reasoned argument, that, as J. Roger puts it, "nothing resembles the realm of chance more than this universe in which everything is rigorously determined by everything. When the dice fall on the baize, they obey the immutable laws of motion. . . . The universe of Diderot is a gigantic game of dice, in which everything is determined, nothing known, and in which the dice themselves change shape during the course of the play."[97] The turbulence of all that is, is governed by the order of law; but that turbulence is a law of disorder. Ultimately, then, the two dialectical opposites are one, and there is no way to extricate the question from the categories of the mind or to separate it from the subjectivity of the perceiving individual.[98]

[97] J. Roger, *Les Sciences de la vie*, p. 663.

[98] My colleague, Prof. Peter Heath, has kindly read this chapter and offered some valuable suggestions. He sees an influence or parallel in Spinoza (determinism and materialism with emphasis on interdependence rather than linear causation, a similar theory of mind, order and disorder viewed as relative and human concepts) and in Hume (a similar idea of natural design in the posthumous *Dialogues* may well have been aired over the dinner table). Diderot struck him as an "enterprising groper," very good at throwing up questions, with "almost too many ideas," but without the patience (or the knowledge) "to sort them out—though he does at times get astonishingly close to what was later to become the received view."

The truth of this last statement has often not been adequately appreciated (although Diderot has sometimes been given too much credit, e.g., for the theory of evolution). Many ideas that Carl Becker attributes specifically to the nineteenth and twentieth century context are in Diderot (the world is not "a neat and efficient machine," man is "a chance deposit," the world is "a continuous flux, a ceaseless and infinitely complicated process of waste and repair . . . of forces parting sooner or later on their way," science deals "with changes of configuration"). (*The Heavenly City of the Eighteenth-Century Philosophers*, New Haven, 1932, pp. 12, 14, 22, 24.) Curiously, a recent television program on the universe proclaimed that the idea that stars, like animals, have a birth, a life, a death, is a very recent notion, as are the ideas that elements combine in space and have a tendency to form complex structures.

II.
Aesthetics

THE QUESTION OF ORDER UNDERLIES many of Diderot's theoretical and practical considerations on the arts. His most abstract effort, the article "Beau," which he wrote for the *Encyclopédie,* is itself the product of an orderly, rigorously schematic intellect. One of its major theses is that the genesis of the aesthetic experience is experimental, not innate; that it is the product of the innate *need* to reorder the data of sense experience for the purpose of satisfying our *needs.*[1] The *modus operandi* of our innate reflective faculties involves the comparison and recombination of perceptions—the artist's work will later be defined by Diderot in just this way. This process is simultaneously cognitive and evaluative. Man's distinctive tool-making ability is precisely an ordering (or a re-ordering) process, one which involves an intuition of relationships, though Diderot does not use the latter phrase at this point.[2]

Writing as a post-Lockean and before Kant's critical philosophy, he affirms that the ideas of order, arrangement, symmetry, proportion, and unity are factitious,

[1] *Oeuvres esthétiques,* ed. P. Vernière, Paris [1959], pp. 415-16.

[2] This origin will lead Diderot to assume a relationship between utility and beauty—the beautiful male body reflects its reproductive function—but he does not, as it is sometimes held, reduce beauty to utility. For his ideas on the relation of the artist to society, see J. L. Waldauer, *Society and Freedom of the Creative Man in Diderot's Thought, Diderot Studies V,* Genève, 1964.

an induction from experience (or, as he puts it, from practice). Only along this pathway does the mind reach the "positive abstract notions" which make up the idea of order, and the negative abstract notions of disorder. For Diderot, this genesis makes them even more real and distinct, and he groups them with our other primary operative ideas: length, width, depth, quantity, number. They are universals. In all places and times, the abstractions which designate "order, proportion, relationships, harmony" are the constituents of the idea of beauty.

It may well seem that in using these words Diderot is indulging in a repetition of quasi-synonyms. Doubtless realizing this, he proceeds to a precise definition which at once synthesizes and clarifies his words. Is there one factor, he asks, present in the variety of objects men call beautiful, and essential to that designation? Is there a factor "with which beauty begins, increases, varies infinitely, declines and disappears"? His reply is affirmative: "only the nature of relationships is capable of these effects."[3] This is the basis in order, but it is not yet a definition. It is only the objective basis for an experience which is, like all experience, subjective. This second notion leads to a complete definition: "I therefore call *beautiful* outside of myself whatever contains in itself that which can awaken the idea of relationships in my understanding; and *beautiful* in relation to me, whatever does awaken that idea." One may perhaps think of Hegel's definition of beauty as "the rational rendered sensible."

Diderot's definition has two advantages. In the first place, it assigns their proper role both to subjectivity, which seeks and experiences order, and to the non-

[3] *Oeuvres esthétiques*, p. 418.

subjective components of order. In the second place, it accounts for the wide diversity of individual taste and cultural differences by making the aesthetic experience dependent, in the last analysis, on the ability to perceive relationships, an ability that depends in turn both on the individual's innate gifts or limits and on the character of the experience with which he has been provided. Diderot offers examples to show that the number or complexity of relationships the individual can grasp and the character of the experiences in which, according to the culture to which be belongs, he will discern relationships or be blind to them constitute the two variables of taste and aesthetic judgment.[4] When the perception of relationships reaches a certain point of complexity and a certain pitch of emotional arousal, we may speak of the sublime. Diderot does not, however, confine the work of art to the beautiful. The important role he gives to the ugly and the distorted—Hegel's "emphatic features of the unbeautiful"—is well known. The sublime more often than not involves this type of relationships, precisely an ordered disorder, as we shall see.

These basic considerations on the nature of beauty and the aesthetic experience are too abstract to be of much service to Diderot the practitioner and critic of the arts. He will supplement them, remaining wherever possible on a level of abstractions and general principles, but with specific problems in mind. The result will be a body of doctrines and precepts which do not make up a consistent system, but are all the richer and more pro-

[4] A more extensive discussion of other aspects of Diderot's views in "Beau" will be found in L. G. Crocker, *Two Diderot Studies*, Baltimore, 1952.

vocative, as Diderot seeks to break through the limits of both neo-classical theory and practice.

Diderot's considerations on genius are on a level not quite so abstract as the article "Beau," but they are often close to it. It is well known that his thinking on this subject changed dramatically. In his early writings, the genius is delineated as an agent of disorder, and as we see in the considerations on Racine in *Le Neveu de Rameau,* Diderot always considered that he may be so in a moral or social sense. In the article "Eclectisme," Diderot exclaims about the enthusiasm, "the disorderly progression and the swervings of poetic genius."[5] The creative mind finds imaginary causes and imaginary effects. The "transport" of the feverish moment enables the poet to perceive new relationships, which no one has ever seen or supposed, among disparate objects. This picture of the creative genius throws down the gauntlet, as Paul Vernière has noted, to the classical sense of measure defended by Voltaire. It is developed further in the article "Génie" (1757), which undoubtedly belongs in part to Diderot. The poet in his frenzy, he there declares, "controls neither the nature nor the order of his ideas" as he flies to extremes—the sublime, the awful, the somber. He may be irregular, defiant of the canons of good taste, of rules, intolerant of all barriers that hinder his flight to the sublime, the pathetic, the great. He has replaced them with his own ideal model, which dictates his taste. The poet is contrasted with the scientist. The latter, cool, patient, and methodical, is the complete master of the order and coherence of his ideas. The former is swept away by the torrent of his, as he is gripped by his dominant characteristic, *sensibilité.* By

[5] *Oeuvres esthétiques,* p. 10.

these demiurgic gifts, he seems to change the nature of things and open up the pathways to the future. "If one forms the object by a choice of scattered parts, which makes the sensation of the imitation stronger than it would have been in nature, one is a poet."[6]

In essence, Diderot's remarks pertain more to the creative process than to the resultant work or to the aesthetic experience it causes—the experience that was the subject of the article "Beau." Diderot does not mean that the work of art is itself disorderly. This conclusion seems justified by the *Eloge de Richardson.* While Diderot is ecstatic about Richardson's attainment of sublime heights of pathos and truth, admiration for the construction of his novels is implied throughout. There is, then, no contradiction with the article "Beau." The genius, working in the way that is his, creates a new order, by his discovery or invention of new relationships and by his ability to state them with technical perfection. As in nature, order arises out of a disorderly, energetic process.

Diderot was to change his stand in later years. In a note, "Sur le génie" (probably written in the middle 1770's), he states that the power of genius does not lie in imagination, judgment, enthusiasm, *sensibilité,* or taste. It is mysterious and undefinable, except for one characteristic, an extraordinary gift for observation, an ability to see what others do not notice. This gift leads to a kind of sixth sense, or "prophetic power," which enables the genius to intuit what will work, in art, and what will not. This mastery, or "olympian power" (as Vernière puts it), is the central notion around which Diderot will later develop a new theory of the creative act, in his famous *Paradoxe sur le comédien* (1773).

[6] *Eléments de physiologie,* p. 236.

The themes of *Le Paradoxe sur le comédien* are too complex and too well known to warrant detailed recapitulation here. Centering on the art of acting, they envelop finally all the arts. Again the creative act or process is the focus of Diderot's speculations. In opposing his earlier concepts of enthusiasm and disordered *sensibilité* (now taken to be the character of the mediocre), it is clear that Diderot, even in the creative process, turns against his pre-romantic admiration for the disorder of raw emotion to re-emphasize the classical value of rationally directed order. "It is not his heart, it is his head that does everything."[7] (He is referring to the genius in all the arts of "imitation of nature.") We can almost glimpse the disembodied M. Teste of Valéry. (In the *Rêve de d'Alembert*, where Diderot expresses similar ideas, he asserts that, if a great man is unfortunately born sensitive, he will bend every effort to weaken and to master that fatal gift and to make the brain sole ruler of his movements.) Enthusiasts or passionate people enact life's comedy, the great artist observes and studies them with icy detachment.

The "ideal model," which a master in any of the creative arts will construct for himself, represents his perception of truth, or relationships. But it is not the product of the quirks of his personality. It is reached by study and intellectual acuity. It is itself a process. This is at once a classical and a rational concept. Order (truth, relationships) is grasped by a well-ordered and orderly mind, which goes beyond the order (or the disorder) of phenomena to the higher level of truth, that is, to a higher or more fundamental order of the universal and permanent to which access is gained through the ideal model.

[7] *Paradoxe, Oeuvres esthétiques*, p. 210.

"But if a crowd of people that some catastrophe has brought together in the street should suddenly display, each one in his own way, their natural emotivity, without having planned anything, they will create a marvelous spectacle, a thousand precious models for sculpture, painting, music and poetry."

"That is so. But would that spectacle be comparable to one resulting from an intelligent concert, from that harmony the artist will introduce when he transports the scene from the street corner to the stage or the canvas? If you assert that, I shall reply: what then is that vaunted magic of art, since it comes down to spoiling what raw nature and a chance arrangement had done better than it? . . . Besides, you are speaking about a real thing, and I am speaking about an imitation; you are speaking of a fleeting instant of nature, and I about a work of art, planned, worked out, which has its development and which endures.[8]

Diderot's favorite and persistent idea of an "ideal model" is not only a Platonic concept that enables the poet or artist to rise above particular accidents to a purer, more general, truer imitation of nature. It carries forward the theory of the article "Beau" by allowing him to escape from pure subjectivity in order to reach the objective elements of beauty, those relationships that may constitute an aesthetic order.

Is man, then, condemned never to agree either with his fellow-men or with himself, about the only matters that are really important for him to know, truth, goodness, beauty? Are these local things, momentary and arbitrary, words empty of meaning? Do they not

[8] Ibid., p. 319.

have any real existence? Is a thing true, good, and beautiful, when it seems so to me? . . .

It is certain that our disputes will be endless as long as each one takes himself as judge. There will be as many measuring sticks as there are men, and the same man will have as many modules as he has appreciably different periods in his life.

It seems to me that this is enough for me to realize the need for seeking a measure, a modulus outside of myself. Until that search has been made, most of my judgments will be false, and all will be uncertain.

But where shall I find the invariable measure I am looking for and do not have? . . . In an ideal man whom I shall form, to whom I shall present objects, who will judge, and of whom I shall be merely the faithful echo? . . . But that man will be my own work. . . . What does it matter, if I create him according to unchanging elements. . . . And these unchanging elements, where are they? . . . In nature? . . . Very well, but how can I assemble them? . . . The thing is difficult, but is it impossible? . . . Even if I could not hope to form a perfect model, am I absolved from trying? . . . No. . . . Then let's try. . . . But if the model of beauty to which the sculptors of antiquity afterwards related all their works required so many observations, studies and labor, what am I committing myself to? . . . Yet I must do that, or always hear myself called Ariste the philosopher, and blush.[9]

Art, continues Diderot, cannot tolerate the cacophony nature sometimes contains.[10]

[9] *De la poésie dramatique,* in *Oeuvres esthétiques,* pp. 284-85.

[10] As I have shown in the aforementioned study, Diderot is far from consistent on this subject.

This separation of art and nature should not be taken to mean that Diderot favored a neat and tidy art. His romantic, often naively melodramatic tastes are well known. He does not abandon them, nor is any contradiction involved. Disorder has its place in the world of art as in the natural world, but its effective aesthetic representation can only be the result of the artist's ordering process: selection, accentuation, composition, a *concordia discors*. The artist feels; but his feeling, instead of degenerating into the confusion of *sensibilité*, becomes part of the material on which his judgment works.[11]

Diderot felt equally at home in the lofty realm of abstract speculation and in the contentious arena of aesthetic criticism. He had turned first to poetry. His *Essai sur les sourds et muets* (1751) is concerned in the first instance with linguistics. His endeavor to distinguish a natural, conventional and scientific order of words in language testifies to his constant preoccupation with problems of order or ordering. I shall not go into the technicalities of this discussion. The use of inversions leads him into poetic theory. In poetry the order of ideas may be reversed for the sake of harmony. Inversion has another value, one which for Diderot is the primary characteristic of poetry, suggestiveness. Nature, truth and imitation are here, as elsewhere, the substance and method of art. But the true poet accomplishes a creative act. The ordering of words is part of his task, but versification and rhyme do not constitute poetry. There is a magic in poetry which arises from the evocative power of sounds and symbols (words and their combinations). The poet possesses the power of turning them into more than what they are by themselves, into "emblems" and "hieroglyphs," opening the door to new

[11] This view is clearly expressed on pp. 372-73.

kinds of sensations and experiences. Poetic emblems have the inexplicable power to express the totality of an event, with its emotional charge, and in its instantaneous, or simultaneous reality; other forms of verbal discourse, being analytical and discursive rather than synthetic, are incapable of this.

Although the following passages are well known, they are significant and original enough to warrant quotation at this point.

> The state of the mind, in an indivisible instant, was represented by a throng of terms required by the precision of language, which distributed a total impression into parts; and because these terms were pronounced sequentially and were heard only as they were pronounced, we were led to believe that the affections of the soul, which they represented, had the same sequence. But it is not that way at all. Our state of mind is one thing; the account we give of it, either to ourselves or to others, is another. The total and instantaneous sensation of that state is one thing; the sequential and detailed attention we are obliged to give it in order to analyze it, express it, and make ourselves understood, is another. Our mind is a moving picture, according to which we are constantly painting. It takes us a considerable time to render it faithfully; but it exists in its entirety, and all at once: the mind does not work like expression, in measured steps. The brush executes only over a period of time what the painter's eye takes in at a single glance.[12]

> We must distinguish, in speech in general, thought and its expression. If the thought is rendered clearly,

[12] *Oeuvres complètes*, I, 369.

> limpidly and precisely, that is enough for familiar conversation. Add to these qualities the choice of terms together with the rhythm and harmony of the phrasing, and you will have the style that suits the pulpit. But you will still be far from poetry, especially the poetry which the ode and the epic poem display in their descriptions. Then there passes into the poet's discourse a spirit that moves and vivifies every syllable of it. What is that spirit? I have sometimes felt its presence; but all I know about it is that it is what causes things to be said and shown all at once; it is what brings it about that at the same time that the understanding grasps them, the soul is moved by them, the imagination sees them and the ear hears them, and that discourse is no longer only a sequence of vigorous terms that express a thought with power and nobility, but that it is, beyond this, a tissue of hieroglyphs heaped upon each other, that paint it. I might say that in this sense all poetry is emblematic.
>
> But the understanding of the poetic emblem is not given to everyone. It is necessary to be almost able to create it in order to feel it strongly.[13]

Samuel Johnson thought that "poetic generality evinces itself as an organization, an ordering of particular details."[14] Diderot would accept and include this definition; he goes beyond it and sets up a realm of peculiar aesthetic experience belonging to poetry alone.

[13] Ibid., I, 374. See also the Introduction of Paul H. Meyer's valuable critical edition of the *Lettre sur les sourds et muets, Diderot Studies VII*, Genève, 1965.

[14] Lionel Basney, "*Lucidus Ordo.* Johnson and Generality," *Eighteenth Century Studies*, vol. 5 (1971), pp. 54-55. For another similarity to Diderot, see p. 50.

Later Diderot turned to the theater, in which he was successful as a theorist and unsuccessful as a practitioner of his own precepts. After *Les Bijoux indiscrets,* his first important dicta on theatrical practice are in the dialogues, *Entretiens sur le Fils naturel* (1757). There, right at the outset, Dorval insists on the importance of a clear ordering of events, in a statement that virtually contains a definition of order as a rational harmony. "I am more concerned with their ordering than with their multiplicity. . . . The art of plotting consists in linking events in such a way that the sensible spectator always sees a satisfying reason in them."[15] Yet disorder must be an important part of all drama, as it is of life. Indeed, it is the substance of dramatic conflict. From the aesthetic viewpoint, order becomes all the more essential to the proper, effective rendition of irrationality. Diderot expounds this point at length. He comments on the proper positioning of actors in the expression of wild passions and tumultuous action, making an explicit analogy with the art of composition in painting.

> Stage action must still be very imperfect, since we see almost no situation on the stage that could be made into an acceptable composition in a painting. What then! Is truth less essential there than on canvas? Can it be a rule, that the artist must be more distant from the thing in proportion as the art is closer to it, and put less verisimilitude into a living scene, in which real men are acting, than into a colored scene, where one sees, so to speak, only their shadows?
>
> As for me, I think that if a dramatic work were

[15] *Oeuvres esthétiques,* p. 81.

> well written and well played, the stage would offer the spectator as many real *tableaux* as the action would have favorable moments for the painter.[16]

Disorder must be displayed with consistency, down to the details of clothing.[17] Similarly, "a dominating taste for order" requires us to establish correct proportions, one exaggeration calling for a similar augmentation of all the rest.[18] Lamenting the impossibility of putting the terror and pity of Aeschylus on the French stage, Diderot attributes it to the fetish of a single action. "In nature there are almost always simultaneous actions, whose concomitant representation, fortifying each other reciprocally, would produce terrible effects on us." But this skill has been lost. The French must await a genius who knows, among other things, how to combine pantomime with discourse without confusion.[19]

Although Diderot was not that genius, he understood how a hidden order, a rational ordering, produces the most telling rendition of emotional disorder. "Dramatic art prepares events only to link them. . . . Art imitates even the subtle manner with which nature conceals the *liaison* of its effects."[20] Ultimately, order depends on the writer's ability to discover true relationships in nature, though nature is only a relative, not an arbitrary limit. This is true of all the arts. Regardless of the type of subject, "the universal order of things . . . must always be the basis of poetic reason." This recapturing of the natural order in the artifact makes any subject valid, and renders such precepts as the unities trivial.[21] Incidentally, Diderot's own classification of the different

[16] Ibid., p. 89. [17] Ibid., p. 91. [18] Ibid., p. 151.
[19] Ibid., pp. 114-15. See also, p. 162.
[20] Ibid., pp. 130-31. [21] Ibid., pp. 160-61.

kinds of plays is itself an exercise in rational discrimination and ordering.[22]

In the subsequent treatise, *Discours sur la poésie dramatique* (1758), Diderot descends into the arena of precept and practice. In a series of chapters, he preaches to the playwright on subjects such as these: "On the Plan and on Dialogue," "On the Outline," "On Incidents," "On Division into Acts," and the like. The details do not concern us here, only Diderot's preoccupation with plan and order.

Unity in Diderot's aesthetic theories lies less in their stability or in a systematic inner consistency than in his efforts to apply them, with proper modifications, to the several arts. The elimination of the arbitrary and the quest for true relations (though not necessarily as found in nature) recur throughout his writings on the fine arts, and are consistent with his attachment to dramatic effect on the canvas as well as on the stage. In the *Essais sur la peinture* (1766), his insistence on perspective and on the modifications of tonality in light and color carry forward these ideas.[23] The organic unity of the aesthetic object requires a careful choice of details, or "accessories," as he says. Constant awareness of subtle relationships and of the association of ideas alone can assure the rational harmony that is requisite to emotional effect, although by itself it does not necessarily produce such an effect, since much depends on human truth, and the subject. If the subject of the canvas is ruins, the accessories may well be a traveler with a pack on his back, a violent wind, a woman carrying a child wrapped in rags, or men on horseback, their faces wrapped in scarves. "Who suggested these accessories? The affinity of ideas. Everything passes away, man, and man's dwelling

[22] Ibid., pp. 136-38.

[23] Ibid., pp. 687-88.

place."[24] If the focus is a tomb, the accessories will change. The traveler and his dog will stop to rest, the woman to suckle her child.

Diderot's last work on painting, the *Pensées détachées* (1776-1781), confirms the persistence of his tenets. "Nothing is beautiful without unity; and there is no unity without subordination . . . and from this subordination comes the harmony which presupposes variety."[25] Again, this idea does not eliminate the portrayal of confusion, or of a great number of unrelated figures and actions, when confusion is appropriate, as in the portrayal of a *kermesse* or a battle scene. But each position, each action must in itself be according to nature.[26]

Throughout the series of *Salons*, the importance of composition in Diderot's eyes becomes increasingly evident. The relationship of figures and objects must be intellectually satisfying to him, and he enjoys communicating this aesthetic experience to the reader.

> It is a very beautiful thing. The painter occupies the middle of the canvas. He is seated: he has his legs crossed and an arm around the back of his chair; he is resting. The sketch of his father's portrait is before him on an easel. His sister is standing behind his armchair. Nothing is more simple, more natural and true than this last figure. The artist's dressing gown gives a marvelous appearance of silk. His arm hanging over the back of the chair seems to be entirely out of the canvas; one has only to go up to it and take it.[27]

The painting is by Van Loo. Boucher often does not fare as well.

[24] Ibid., p. 709. [25] Ibid., p. 760. [26] Ibid., pp. 784-85.

[27] *Oeuvres complètes*, ed. Assézat-Tourneux, X, 168.

> But what do this vase and its pedestal signify? And those heavy overhanging branches? When one writes, must one write everything? When one paints, must one paint everything?[28]

> And then, a confusion of objects heaped upon each other, so out-of-place, so ill-assorted, that it is less a sensible man's painting than a madman's dream.[29]

Again he scores Boucher's shortcoming:

> Those subtle, fine analogies that on a canvas require putting objects next to each other and that tie them together with secret and imperceptible threads, by God! he doesn't know what all that is. All his compositions make an unbearable din to the eyes.[30]

Doyen's "Miracle des Ardents" is no better: "all these objects compose a chaos, a compact mass of figures."[31] Not so with a work of Robert's: "It is an infinite variety of picturesque objects, without confusion; it is an enchanting harmony."[32] The excess represents disorder, because the mind is unable to discern relationships. Greuze never makes this mistake. Diderot's description of "Piété filiale" is too long to repeat, but we may note one or two key sentences:

> Even the background reminds us of the care they are taking of the old man. . . . The number of characters assembled in a rather small space is very large; nevertheless, they are there without confusion, for this master excels above all in ordering his scene.[33]

[28] Ibid., X, 172.
[29] *Oeuvres esthétiques*, p. 454.
[30] *Oeuvres complètes*, X, 257.
[31] Ibid., XI, 175.
[32] Ibid., XI, 240.
[33] Ibid., X, 209.

Diderot most often begins his translation of a painting into words by giving an account of the position of the figures and objects and of the utilization of space, or the proper assemblage of observed details. He will then go on to action, gesture and expression, culminating in the principal value: dramatic and emotional effect, and mood (what Gombrich calls the arousal value of art). This order is not always followed, but these elements, plus drawing and color, and finally, moral value, compose his aesthetic world.

Mood and emotion may, we have seen, require disorder; but such disorder, unlike that of Boucher, is apparent, in the sense of being a calculated effect, recalling Boileau's principle, "A fine disorder is the finest effect of art." Monotony and symmetry prevent the little surprises and the variety that move us. Thus a painting by Fragonard prompts this exclamation: "It is a small *tour de force*, this white dog placed in front and in the bright light."[34] For Diderot, one of the masters of the art of skillful disorder is Vernet, whose rendition of a storm at sea fills him with ecstasy because, by capturing the frantic action on shipboard, it conveys the dreadful emotion of the event.[35]

Disgusted by one of Hallé's compositions, Diderot redoes it on paper (a frequent practice of his), in such a way that the groupings and expressions would arouse emotion.[36] The following article, on another work of Hallé, makes it clear that meaning grows out of the relationships established by the composition. This is again obvious when he suggests to Greuze the meaningful order of bodies, hands, and clothing which would compose a painting to be entitled "Le Modèle honnête"

[34] Ibid., X, 409. [35] Ibid., X, 201. [36] Ibid., X, 266.

(a suggestion taken up not by Greuze but by Baudouin).[37] Aesthetic disorder results when no significant relation can be found. "That young man with his elbows on the table—what is he doing there? I have no idea. What about that *abbé*? Again I have no idea. What does that lackey who is leaving signify?"[38] Or about another painting, "They are saying that this picture is well composed. But what is a composition in which, out of seven characters, four are superfluous?"[39] He expresses his view most pithily in the *Salon de 1767*: "No matter how these animate objects are arranged next to each other, I shall say that they are grouped only when they are tied together by a common function" (XI, 41). And again, in another way, when he warns that the artist must have the courage to reject incompatible accessory ideas, no matter how interesting. If he does not, "an accessory idea imposes itself on the whole, instead of receiving its meaning from it." A great master has this courage.[40] On the other hand, a richly detailed composition that keeps its organic unity heightens values.[41] It can create the sensation of motion, such as a march, or of action. But the law of harmony tells us that movement must be in inverse proportion to the gravity of the personages: "in the physical realm, it is the law of masses; in the moral, it is the law of character. . . . Expressions, whatever they may be, passions and movement diminish in proportion as the models are more exaggerated." Raphael, far from being cold, is a genius precisely because

> he makes the expressions, the movement, the passions, the actions proportionate to the model he has im-

[37] Ibid., XI, 74. [38] Ibid., X, 269. [39] Ibid., X, 277.

[40] Ibid., XI, 340, also pp. 40-41.

[41] Ibid., X, 296-97, 326-28.

> agined and chosen. . . . There is a middle point between coldness and extravagance, and that point is the one at which, relatively to the action that is represented, the choice of models is combined, for the greatest possible advantage, with the quality of movement.[42]

Even when there is only one major figure, as in Greuze's "La Jeune Fille qui pleure son oiseau mort," Diderot pays great attention to the placing and relationships of the body. According to his theory of the unity of the body, a person's age, deformities, work, or condition (such as pregnancy) set up changes throughout the body, and alter the relationships of the parts. Thinking of the painter's problems, he writes: "All the parts of the body have their own expression. . . . Expression, like blood and the fibres of the nervous system, winds and manifests itself throughout a figure."[43]

Nowhere are these preoccupations and values brought out more clearly than in his analyses of two sketches by Greuze, "La Mère bien-aimée" and "Le Fils ingrat."[44] About the latter he summarizes, "Everything is intelligently worked out, ordered, characterized, and clear in this sketch." A good artist, he comments in discussing Vernet, is compelled to put that cloud exactly where it is, because it establishes the planes of the picture.[45] Returning to the subject of battle scenes, he admits that they are outside the rules of the unities of time, place, and action. Yet the essential aesthetic unity of organic structure is not lost thereby. "It is a spectacle composed

[42] Ibid., XI, 36-37.

[43] *Pensées détachées, Oeuvres esthétiques*, p. 798.

[44] *Oeuvres complètes*, X, 351-56.

[45] Ibid., XI, 101.

of a diversity of incidents that imply no contradiction. . . . Terror and pity must rush at me from every point on the canvas."[46] The artist's freedom to create, to see and make us see new relationships is a vital part of Diderot's theory. Vernet can teach us to see in nature what we are not able to. "How many things you would find to correct in nature! How many art would eliminate, that spoil the ensemble and harm the effect; how many it would bring together, that would double our enchantment!" What this passage says is that nature's order is aesthetically imperfect, haphazard even when effective. What nature lacks is an aim or directing purpose (compare Kant's aesthetic teleology) and a self-critical awareness. These the artist must have, in addition to technique. Nature is the subject of imitation, but art is creative, a process of *perfectionnement,* as Diderot has explained in his theory of the ideal model.

The aesthetic experience, for Diderot, is not autonomous and self-enclosed. It is a reaction to the natural, metaphysical, and moral world. It can never stray far from nature's norm, though it is not nature. The emotion it inspires does not come directly from the creator's own emotion, but from his representation of reality, or its appearance, in his conscious production of new constructive syntheses. Although in one sense it is a harmony with nature, springing from an intuition of significant form, in another sense it supplants nature, even as tools do. In the creative act the raw material of natural relationships is transmuted. Man is carried beyond nature, though never outside of the natural, into a new focus, or a new formation that might never exist in nature. In the extension of experience on the plane

[46] Ibid., XI, 271.

of formal invention, the relationships of the new structure are imagined, not perceived.

External order and disorder are not controlling factors in this accomplishment. That which, in human terms, is disorder, may be aesthetically valid, and in its emotional values, more valid than order. It may also be more valid in moral terms, but this is not necessarily so. Through selection and reordering—the imaginative and purposeful recombination of possible relationships—the mind creates its own order, even an order of disorder. One scholar writes of Diderot: "He admits through non-form that form, order, reason [do] not exist in the world."[47] The statement is accurate, but not adequate as a generalization. The same writer adds that he "selects what he will include and thereby forms his work towards an effect." Indeed, "non-form" is a part of a plotted aesthetic illusion, just as is realism.

It should be evident that Diderot's aesthetics contain both Platonic and Aristotelian elements.[48] In the notion of the ideal model, the artist's own mind replaces, or corresponds to, a permanent truth that is non-existent in the sensual world, and which, in the Platonic tradition, alone has objective reality. In the last analysis, it is an inner vision. On the other hand, like Aristotle, Diderot emphasizes technique and the realization of potential form. He unites the perceptual and the conceptual vision; the poet's and the artist's work is both representa-

[47] S. L. Kabelac, "Irony as a Metaphysics in *Le Neveu de Rameau*," *Diderot Studies XIV*, p. 105. A similar idea was earlier expressed by me in my article, "*Jacques le Fataliste*, an 'expérience morale,'" *Diderot Studies III*, Genève, 1961, pp. 73-99.

[48] It is well known that Diderot had read Plato and Aristotle thoroughly. See *inter alia*, Donal O'Gorman, *Diderot the Satirist*, Toronto, 1971.

tional and creative. In fact, although his statements on literal or interpretative imitation are sometimes contradictory,[49] his basic view of literary realism and *vraisemblance* makes imitation, in a way, more apparent than real. Illusion is the goal, and it is a requisite for emotional effect. Art is a lie, blended with truth. It not only discovers, it intensifies.

Although Diderot does not attempt to reduce the motives of aesthetic experience or of creative aesthetic activity to specific factors, such as the demiurgic impulse, play, or intensification of existence, elements such as these seem to be implied. Art, for Diderot, is the peculiarly human manifestation of the universal and omnipresent law that governs all natural processes, the tendency to bring into being ordered and more complex structures. It expresses our need to order and re-order experience, to reproduce and to reinvent it, in order to contemplate, understand, enjoy and intensify it. Art is a peculiarly human reaction to the world, one which is centered on orderly and disorderly relationships as they are perceived and re-created. Much of experience is one of disorder, or apparent disorder. But, as we have seen, even disorder consists of relationships and so requires of the artist a conscious and controlled ordering process. The artist's task is further conceived as the re-creation and communication of beauty, truth and emotion, never of pure form in and for itself. Although beauty (somewhat as Kant was to say) is an independent experience, and aesthetic value is not reducible to extra-aesthetic considerations, the concrete reality of art—a painting, a poem—involves significates, affects, function, moral value, as well as aesthetic judgment and taste. That is to

[49] See index to Crocker, *Two Diderot Studies*, under "Imitation."

say, art is inconceivable, to Diderot, without the values of arousal and of statement. In art, enjoyment, interpretation, and evaluation have broader human and social dimensions than the aesthetic experience itself; and they should have. Aesthetic creation is not a solipsistic activity, but a form of communication, with content and consequences; it embodies, reflects and heightens the appreciation of order and disorder, in all spheres.

In the first part of this study, we saw that order and disorder are simultaneous cosmic realities, and that it is difficult to disentangle the subjective and objective elements in those notions. In the next two parts we shall see that in the human world, too, the demand for order, except in art, is a hopeless quest, frustrated by equally natural and powerful drives toward disorder in the moral and social spheres. In the human world, as in the natural and the aesthetic, order and disorder play an endless, dynamic game. Art alone, by creating its own peculiarly human reality, enables man to triumph over disorder, to satisfy his deep emotional and intellectual need for order. In the very deepest sense, aesthetic creation is an unconscious defiance, a protest against destruction. I am not sure how clearly Diderot realized this, or whether he realized it at all, except in the more obvious sense of the desire to survive in the memory of later generations. But to us, in the twentieth century, this idea seems a significant part of what he is saying.

III.
Morals

ONE MIGHT THINK THAT IN DIDEROT'S mind the question of moral order and disorder should follow hard upon the cosmic considerations. Even given a morally neutral or value-free universe, this is not necessarily so, except for the nihilist who rejects the validity of conventional or man-made limits. While Diderot indulges in moments of speculation in the vein of moral nihilism that was so present in the minds of the *philosophes,* cosmic referents play a rather small role in his ethical explorations after the *Lettre sur les aveugles* (1749). Even there they really form a background designed precisely to exclude them and to establish the biological and social genesis of moral values. This is done indirectly, following his favorite method, by exploring abnormal or extreme cases. In the *Lettre sur les aveugles,* his approach is through the psychology of the blind. The resultant relativism, it must be noted, is not taken as a sign of disorder. On the contrary, the *Lettre* brings out a strong thrust on the part of all men, subjected to communal living and determined by their organic constitution, to impose order in their relationships. The validity of the order so established is not questioned.

This validity is argued explicitly and vigorously, even somewhat desperately, in the article "Droit naturel" in the *Encyclopédie.* In this important piece, Diderot brings into the open the arguments of the moral anarchist and attempts to refute them. Other writers, such as Voltaire and Saint-Hyacinthe, had also done this, endeavoring to substitute a deistic, naturalistic, or social foundation for the discarded Christian scheme.[1] The anarchist's argument in "Droit naturel" is a succinct résumé of that of all moral nihilists in the eighteenth century, including La Mettrie and Sade. Even the defenders of morality, such as d'Holbach, accepted it as a basic postulate and problem.

> I feel that I am bringing terror and confusion among mankind; but I must either be unhappy or make others unhappy; and no one is dearer to me than I am to myself. Let no one reproach me for this abominable predilection; it is not free. It is the voice of nature, which never expresses itself more strongly in me than when it speaks to me in my own favor. . . . Is there one amongst you who, on the point of death, would not buy back his life at the expense of the greater part of the human race. . . ? If my happiness demands that I get rid of all lives that are importunate to me, then an individual, whoever he may be, must also be able to get rid of mine if it vexes him. Reason demands it, I subscribe to it. I am not so unjust as to require of another the sacrifice that I am not ready to make to him.[2]

[1] See the ninth chapter of Voltaire's *Traité de métaphysique*, ed. H. T. Patterson, Manchester, 1937; and L. G. Crocker, "Saint-Hyacinthe et le nihilisme moral," *Revue d'Histoire littéraire de la France*, vol. 64 (1964), pp. 462-66.

[2] *Oeuvres complètes*, XIV, 298. While part of "Droit naturel" was probably taken from a source or sources unknown, this development has the stamp of Diderot's own vigorous dialectic. Moreover, similar ideas are expressed by him in a contemporaneous work, the *Apologie de l'abbé de Prades* (ibid., I, 467).

Diderot clearly sees the nihilist as a force of disorder, and therefore as intolerable. He perceives him as a clear and present danger, and accepts the challenge to put him down. He also recognizes, but attributes little weight to, the subjective intuition of natural law. The strategy of his refutation is to insist that the nihilist is obliged to seek the truth, on the penalty of giving up his human status, which would justify exterminating him like a wild beast. This obligation is, in fact, implicitly conceded by his hypothetical antagonist in the very fact of his self-justification. Self-justification is a tacit admission of the obligation to be just. The determination of what is just, Diderot then argues, lies not with the individual, but with the general will of mankind, that is, in natural law, "an order of knowledge and ideas peculiar to the human species, which emanate from its dignity and constitute it."

This is a noble and humanistic declaration. It means that morality is the human right, the human process of imposing order upon the disorderly natural vitalities of the individual. It asserts that morality and society are inseparable. It upholds the superiority of the social, but without crushing the individual. Unfortunately, the abstractness of Diderot's approach, which is so characteristic of eighteenth-century speculation, "fails to come to grips with the existential claims, experiences, and realities of both individual and social life."[3] Years later, arguing in a rather similar fashion in his unpublished *Réfutation d'Helvétius* (1773), Diderot asserts that he is not giving arbitrary or tyrannical power to society, but that moral law rests on the nature of things, that is, on the nature of man who is a moral being. And in his commentary on Hemsterhuis he claims that the material-

[3] L. G. Crocker, *Nature and Culture*, Baltimore, 1963, p. 56.

ists base the ideas of right and wrong on "the eternal relationships" among men—an idea that apparently does not exclude wide variations.[4] From statements such as these, it follows that the nihilist cannot properly appeal, as he always does, from culture to nature.[5]

We shall not here discuss Rousseau's important refutation of Diderot's "Droit naturel" in the second chapter of the first draft of the *Contrat social.*[6] Suffice it to say that he destroys Diderot's argument and comes to grips with the problem on an existential rather than an abstract level. Both the problem and its solution are, for Rousseau, political. Men and society must be remade so that there *are* no nihilists. As Hume also recognized, rational argumentation and persuasion are futile.

[4] *Commentaire sur la* "Lettre sur l'homme et ses rapports" *d'Hemsterhuis,* in *Oeuvres complètes,* ed. Roger Lewinter (Paris, 1971), XI, 10, 69.

[5] There is an interesting similarity between the situation Diderot posits in this argument and the comment of Stuart Hampshire on John Rawls' *A Theory of Justice,* Cambridge, Mass., 1971: "The objection can be made . . . that a blind chooser might, not irrationally, just choose to gamble, and prefer a social order where the winner takes all, or virtually all; he may prefer to take the risk of being a slave if he has a chance of being a master" *(New York Review of Books,* February 24, 1972, p. 37). In other words, the rationality of choosing fairness cannot be proven. Diderot, who was not an intuitionist, does not believe there to be a special power or source of moral knowledge or judgment outside of reflection. Obligation arises from a man's position as a rational member of society. While he elsewhere seems to believe (especially in his plays and fiction) that each person would have a feeling about how decent human beings should behave toward each other, even outside a social order, this possibility does not fit into the rather narrow argumentation in "Droit naturel."

[6] See L. G. Crocker, *Rousseau's Social Contract: An Interpretive Essay,* Cleveland, 1968, pp. 50-55.

In Diderot's published writings for and about the theater, in the personage of "Moi" in *Le Neveu de Rameau,* in his unpublished *Salons,* and in some of his letters, he is the reputedly typical bourgeois of his time, fearful of social disorder, ever on guard to preserve order by tireless moralizing and sentimental preaching about the joys of virtue and the miseries of vice. Diderot's intellectual rebelliousness gets its revenge in his more radical unpublished writings. In what Rousseau properly called the "doctrine secrète," Diderot ranges far and wide. Having expounded a systematic materialism in *Le Rêve de d'Alembert,* Dr. Bordeu establishes moral determinism.[7] The merits of the argument are disputable, but there is no doubt that for Diderot it constitutes a principle of order, set up to eliminate a contrary principle of disorder, namely, free will as he conceived it, that is, the so-called freedom of indifference, which would place man, and man alone, outside the universal law of cause-effect. He does not flinch before the consequences. Virtue and vice have no real existence, Bordeau states, in the sense that acts are not inherently charged with moral value; they are viewpoints, those of society and the individuals affected by our actions. Virtue becomes *bienfaisance,* and society's laws alone eliminate the man who is *malheureusement né* ("unfortunately endowed"). Remorse and self-esteem are "puerilities," punishments are society's self-protective devices, unconnected to any pure or abstract moral justification. These ideas had been expressed earlier by La Mettrie, whom Diderot and other materialists, who believed in the social necessity of morals and wished also to project a favorable image of themselves for strategic reasons, condemned as a fomenter of public disorder. However,

[7] *Oeuvres philosophiques,* pp. 362-64.

Diderot's argument is unique in one important respect. It is quite consistent with his general philosophy of cosmic order and disorder which we examined earlier. Every structure—in this case, the artificial social organism—is impelled by the universal law of process (and so is "justified") to strive to preserve itself against the countervailing forces of disintegration.

Truth is never dangerous, Bordeu now declares. But Diderot bequeathed his unpublished secret doctrine to a future generation, since he knew it would be dangerous to him, and perhaps to the welfare of society.

He did the same with his rather shallow critique of civilized societies in the *Supplément au Voyage de Bougainville* (1772). The sexual restrictions which he publicly upheld as necessary to the moral-social order are here, in a complete reversal, given an antithetical evaluation. Sexual restrictions foment disorder, since they are ineffective and only promote rebellion by an impulse overwhelming in its power. They ruin morality by attaching moral ideas to the sexual act, which is as morally neutral as any other biological bodily process. There is no relation between sexual continence on the part of either sex and public utility, the sole basis of moral law, unless a woman cannot breed. "Vices and virtues, are all equally natural."[8] In other words, they exist because men confer value on acts.

Usually, Diderot defends this conferral of value by society as legitimate, since the universe contains no ordering principles for human affairs, and nature (as "Lui," for instance points out) provides each individual with different directives for self-realization. In his own moralizing to his daughter, in his theater and art criticism, he is quite conventional. In the *Supplément*, how-

[8] Ibid., p. 507.

ever, Diderot, in one of his more anarchical moods, is attempting to establish an identity between nature and culture, one that would perforce exclude social evaluations which contradict such natural impulses as he assumes to be without social import. Thus, to confer value on sexual actions is harmful, because it sets up a division within each person between nature's commands and those of society, "a continual war" between natural man and "artificial, moral man."[9] Jealousy, adultery, incest—crimes of all sorts—are the result of such restrictions as chastity and marriage. In other words, these crimes would not exist if they were not declared to be crimes, if private satisfactions were not made into public offenses. Those unfortunate creatures who do obey the code are the instruments of their own torment and unhappiness, the inevitable result of stifling the voice of nature. "The empire of nature cannot be destroyed."

Unlike so many of Diderot's writings whose contradictions are dialectical and exploratory, the *Supplément au Voyage de Bougainville* contains built-in contradictions that he is trying to escape and cannot master.

Let us consider three major points: sexual activity is outside the sphere of morals (the subtitle of the dialogue and a major thread of its argument); sexual activity has a social function and can be regulated; morality exists in relation to society. It is obvious that the three propositions inevitably conflict. Society does regulate sex on Tahiti in the name of social utility, and social utility is the basis of morality; it follows that society regulates sex in the name of morality, of what is right and wrong. Therefore sexual activity is not outside of moral judgment.

On the one hand, instinctual satisfaction is justifiable

[9] Ibid., p. 511.

in the name of nature and happiness. On the other hand, sexual intercourse, if a woman is either sterile or past child-bearing, is not justifiable in the name of nature and happiness. Is Diderot saying that it is not natural for a woman to have intercourse if she cannot reproduce to provide sons for her country? Or that society (law and morality) intervenes to overrule nature at this point? The latter, beyond doubt. Thus the impulses which are natural and proper, and not subject to restriction by moral or legal codes, are suddenly deprived of all those virtues, even though they continue to be operative in the female body and mind. Incest is fine, if one has a taste for it; but normal embraces become immoral and illegal. This line of reasoning ultimately amounts to the justification—and restriction—of sexual activity in the name of its reproductive function. Such a position is, in this important regard, identical with the Christian view, but contrary to the naturalistic view, in this work and *Le Rêve de d'Alembert*, which makes of any expression of sexual energy a legitimate form of pleasure-seeking.

A second contradiction lies in Diderot's ideas of nature and of the function of law and morality. Nature, he asserts in the *Supplément*, in contradiction to many statements in other writings, always tells us to act in favor of the general interest (p. 482). Conversely, a proper law cannot contravene nature (or else we have the conflict of codes he decries). The distinction between "nature," morality, and proper law is thus effectively obliterated. In this step, rather than in unrestricted sexual activity, lies the anarchistic element. Not only is post-menopausal sex legislated out as "unnatural" (and thus immoral and illegal); but also such a law would be improper if it were not sanctioned by nature. Morality and law are denied their real function as countervailing forces to nature. Yet Diderot knew well that nature inspires anti-social drives and aggressions, and he often says that everyone's happiness cannot be satisfied in the same way. We shall see that he often puts the individual first.

The *Supplément au Voyage de Bougainville* represents a weak utopian effort to harmonize natural and social codes. Of course, laws should, as he says, be based on "nature" (common needs); but they must also limit, discipline, and even contravene nature. In *Mme. de la Carlière* we see the opposition between an ideal and nature (needs); the decision is in nature's favor. The *Supplément* continues this theme. What must be recovered, if men are to be happy, is the natural element that society has repressed. But Diderot, afraid of disorder, tries to save moral and social prerogatives and withdraws from extreme positions at the end. He knows that, in morals and in law, both the individual and society are involved—there exists the need for happiness and the need for order. The former, all too often, represents disorder. Contradictory demands and values are at issue; contradictory truths may and do coexist: this is the problem with which Diderot is grappling. In a letter to Sophie Volland (July 31, 1762), he writes: "In truth, I believe that Nature has no care for right or wrong; she is entirely concerned with two ends: self-preservation of the individual and propagation of the species." Morality is a human work, "natural" to man alone. It separates and alienates him from nature, and defies nature. But in the *Supplément*, Diderot tells us that "civil law must be only the enunciation of nature's law" (*Oeuvres philosophiques*, p. 505). And he says that some things are good and bad "according to nature," a fact that it is not in the power of society to change (pp. 481-82); and also that they are good or bad according to the general (rather than individual) utility. The position is scarcely coherent.

Diderot is on treacherous ground, for the price of civilization is such a war as he describes, between culture and nature.[10] The idea that sexual disorder is conducive to order was too paradoxical. This manuscript, too, remained in Diderot's drawer.

The most significant of Diderot's explorations of the moral world of man derive their originality in large part from the fact that they are carried out in some sort of novelistic form. I have called them moral experiments, and they are simultaneously aesthetic experiments. The artist, we have seen, must create new structures, new ways of ordering reality in a different mode. The structure cannot be independent of meaning, that is, of the thrust of the moral experiment, which realizes itself through that structure. Entranced with "monsters" and the abnormal, Diderot explores the psyche on the extreme edges of its possibilities. In these works moral ideas and problems are expressed through aesthetic form, by their symbolization in concrete images, and through form itself.

The short tales contain the most elementary structures. *Les Deux amis de Bourbonne* (1770) is an apologue, almost a fairy tale.[11] Its two heroes are simple, unspoiled, close to nature and natural goodness. The

[10] Rousseau had proposed an antithetical way to overcome the split between nature and culture.

[11] Diderot changes perspective and narrative technique after the death of Felix, to return later to the tone of a fable. There are serious defects of technique and tone in this tale.

unspoken moral is in part that the order of innocence has no possible home in the man-created order of law, a corrupt, defective order. It is not openly challenged by Diderot, but it is regretted, as superseding something better. But the social order is largely in the background. It is not responsible for the bizarre concatenation of circumstances that govern the lives of the simple characters. As in a naturalistic novel, they seem to us like puppets, helpless in the hands of forces they neither control nor understand. Life as we know it is a kind of moral disorder, a supremely ironical mockery in which goodness is made the sport of the gods. In the famous postscript about realism and novelistic illusion, Diderot makes clear the unity of his thinking on this aspect of aesthetic technique, by likening them to the method he prefers in painting: the combination of the ideal model and the characteristic detail.

In *Ceci n'est pas un conte* (1772), the aesthetic ordering is equally simple, but quite different. I am referring to the principal strategy of the work, not to the tactical details of technique. However, order is again a function of meaning, as Diderot considered it proper for it to be. And the meaning is again closely related to the question of order. Dieckmann sees the theme as the contradiction between "the will for permanence and constancy at the bottom of every love" and the fleeting nature of love.[12] This is indeed one of the themes, and precisely the one related to Diderot's treatment of the same theme in the *Supplément* and *Mme. de la Carlière*. But the impact of *Ceci n'est pas un conte* comes from its plurality of meanings. The tale is in the form of a dyptich. Each panel is, in essence, though not of course in detail, the mirror image of the other. We have two cases of the

[12] H. Dieckmann, *Cinq leçons sur Diderot*, Genève, 1959, p. 73.

domination and exploitation of one sex by the other, two instances of wickedness and ingratitude. There are two panels, because there are two sexes, and either may play the Sadian roles of tyrant and victim. For the stronger partner—the one who does not love—the other is only an object and is treated as such. But there is a further reach. In an orderly disposition of things, Mme. Reymer and Gardeil, the two heartless exploiters, would be paired; whatever their fate, they would at least understand each other. This was precisely what Laclos was to do with Valmont and Mme. de Merteuil. The victims, the gentle, self-sacrificing Tanié and Mlle. de la Chaux, would also form a couple that would represent an eminently satisfying order. But life all too often deals us the wrong cards. The point is emphasized when the narrator remarks about the friend of Mlle. de la Chaux, Dr. Le Camus: "The passion he had acquired for that young woman differed little from the one she felt for Gardeil."[18] The doctor and she would also have made a true couple. But we do not fall in love with the right person. Passion and reason do not accompany each other. Tanié dies, and the heartless Mme. Reymer goes on to richer conquests. Mlle. de la Chaux dies, and Gardeil enjoys wealth, reputation—and is happy. Diderot knows that the virtue-happiness equation which he, d'Holbach, and others proclaimed in their moralistic writings is not a fact of life. It is not so because the impersonal determinism that drives us does not work out in a way that corresponds to our notions of moral value and justice. We may prefer to say again that the gods make sport of us.

> But that's about typical. If there is a good, honest Tanié, providence sends him to a Reymer. If there is

[18] Diderot, *Quatre contes*, ed. J. Proust, Genève, 1964.

a good, honest de la Chaux, she will fall to the lot of a Gardeil, so that all should be for the best.[14]

Like Voltaire, Diderot finds that the only answer to cosmic disorder is the human weapon of irony. To seek for absolutes, to insist fanatically on abstract ideals, is to become the cause of another kind of disorder. And that is the main theme of another tale, *Mme. de la Carlière* (1772).

The absolute on which Mme. de la Carlière insists, at a gathering of friends on the eve of her wedding, is to be the unique object of her husband's sexual interests. "You will be everything in the world for me, but I must be everything in the world for you, I cannot be satisfied with less."[15] If he violates his pledge, she promises, she will not complain, but will die, and see to it that he is covered with disgrace. "I intend to acquire you and to acquire you without reservations." The Chevalier Desroches, her fiancé, takes the vow in good faith. Two years later, he breaks his oath, in part at least out of altruistic motives.[16] When his wife discovers his liaison, she keeps her promise. She speaks no word of complaint. Her health declines. Then, in a *coup de théâtre,* she brings together the same friends and dramatically denounces her husband. While disapproving Desroches' infidelity, the friends expect an ultimate reconciliation. But Mme. de la Carlière leaves her husband, and will never again see him. She burns his letters. Even priestly intervention cannot change her mind. Her deep depression hastens her death, which arouses public execration of a man who has killed his wife.

One of Diderot's purposes is to show the "inconséquence du jugement public," as Naigeon entitled the *conte,* the irresponsibility of the judgments we make of

[14] Ibid., p. 100. [15] Ibid., p. 112. [16] Ibid., p. 117.

others. Several themes are thus interwoven. The sexual infraction is considered in itself as "a trivial misdeed." Both the law of nature in us and the actual practices of society make it trivial; that is, both stand in contradiction to the moral rules of society and religion. These rules are wrong, because they do not work, and so (as the *Supplément au Voyage de Bougainville* brings out) create situations of conflict, guilt, and hypocrisy. Not only Desroches, Diderot would have us think, but few men could satisfy Mme. de la Carlière's fanatical absolute. Our judgment of others, always based on inadequate knowledge, is always irresponsible. This truth is dramatically symbolized, in the introductory portion of the tale, when Desroches, then a magistrate, having condemned a man to death without knowing the reality of his crime, tears up his gown.

Mme. de la Pommeraye (in *Jacques le Fataliste*) and Mme. de la Carlière are comparable women. Both belong to the category of "monsters"—moral monsters—such as Diderot always preferred for his intellectual explorations and experiments. They may be so called because their uncompromising integrity of character leads them to extreme actions of which average men and women would be incapable. To Diderot, Mme. de la Carlière's preference of self-destruction to a lower, unacceptable order of existence is the sign of "greatness in being," even though he disapproves of her outlook as much as he does that of Rameau's nephew.

Diderot's first important novel, *La Religieuse* (1760), explores a realm of disorder which was of particular interest to him, sexual aberrations.[17] In the radical writ-

[17] See Aram Vartanian, "Erotisme et philosophie chez Diderot," *Cahiers de l'Association internationale des études françaises*, No. 13, Paris, 1961, pp. 367-90.

ings of his "secret doctrine," he constantly condemned the repression of natural sexual instincts in Christian civilization. *Mme. de la Carlière* and the *Supplément au Voyage de Bougainville* are variations on the same problem. *La Religieuse,* an earlier work, did not deal with abstractions, but with the institution of monasticism, more exactly with the custom of the *vocation forcée* that played an important role in the *order* of eighteenth-century society. The example of Diderot's unhappy sister had taught him a moving lesson about the possible effects of the cloister on the psychic equilibrium. The real-life case of Marguerite Delamarre enabled him to enlarge the question.[18] The nun of *La Religieuse,* like her real prototype, is not seeking sexual fulfillment, but the freedom of her person and her personality. Her persistence in this quest leads to the releasing of the sadistic instincts in one of the Mothers Superior and the other nuns. The moral and physical tortures so realistically described by Diderot make *La Religieuse* one of the first examples of the Gothic novel (though it was not published until 1796). Among other nuns, repression leads to the perverted outlet of lesbianism, and even to madness. What are we to think of a "social order" which rests in part on an institution productive of the deepest and cruelest disorders in human terms? To what extent can civilization repress and deny nature? These are the questions Diderot raises and explores, in dramatic and pathetic fashion.

The accomplishment of the goals of realism, pathos, and drama was an aesthetic problem of which Diderot was acutely aware, and he himself comments on them. The composition and structure of this novel also raise

[18] See Georges May, *Diderot et "La Religieuse,"* New Haven and Paris, 1954, especially ch. III.

problems for the critic which are beyond the scope of this study. It is enough to note that the general structure chosen by Diderot is one of linear progression; that is, of a clear and evident aesthetic order. The first-person narration sets forth the circumstances leading to monastic incarceration, thence to episodes in a series of convents, each of which presents a further reach of moral corruption in the environment and a greater distress or unhappiness for the victim. Flight and death provide a rapid and unsatisfactory ending, resulting in part from the peculiar circumstances of the composition of the work, and in part from the accomplishment of the author's objective before the dénouement. As in his literary model, Richardson's *Clarissa*, the well-planned accumulation and intensification of episodes is the aesthetic order that dramatically exposes the devastation of behavioral disorders and provides an effective didactic medium.

Le Neveu de Rameau (original version 1762) portrays disorder in an entirely different way. Once again, moral and social disorder are simultaneously implicated, and the tableaux involve psychological disorientations. However, both the aesthetic treatment and the perspective are quite dissimilar from Diderot's other fictional writings. It would appear that for the first time he conceived the idea of achieving an aesthetic unity of content and form. We know little about the conception and composition of the work, but we can at all events affirm that he has achieved such a fusion, and this is not the least of reasons for the greatness of *Le Neveu de Rameau,* for its elusive complexity, and the ever enhanced critical evaluation of its worth.

Aesthetic unity is achieved by the incorporation of the principle of disorder, which is the theme of the work, into its structure. The history of critical evaluations of *Le Neveu de Rameau* is most interesting in this regard. Early readers were struck, or perplexed, by the apparent disorderliness of its form, by its lack of structure. More recent analysis reveals the carefully plotted interweaving of the episodic debates and pantomimes. The background of Diderot's aesthetic theory offers a plausible explanation for this history. We have seen how in his criticism of paintings he recognizes the value of a calculated disorder in the treatment of certain subjects. And his subject here is precisely various forms of disorder.

The use of the dialogue form is admirably suited to this effect. On the one hand, its free movement is conducive to randomness and absence of linear structure. On the other hand, it allows a new dimensionality not found in either the confessional or the epistolary novel. The essential new dimension is that of confrontation, of immediate give-and-take. The theme of order and disorder, complex and elusive as Diderot contemplates it, is explored in its fullest reaches, cosmic, social, and moral, as two antagonistic philosophical outlooks, embodied in the uncompromisingly complex and contradictory personalities of the antagonists, are pitted against each other.

Several points bear emphasis. Diderot maintains at all times complete aesthetic control of a remarkably dynamic encounter, one which seems to meander in the play of free association. Each disjuncture, each fresh tack, performs the role of a new mirror, thus providing the constellated fragments which the reader is summoned to reassemble into a meaningful whole, despite the purely apparent refusal of the organic wholeness that Diderot always recognized as aesthetically indispensable.

Overt unity would have reduced *Le Neveu de Rameau* from an aesthetic and psychological masterpiece to a formal debate, with a total lack of correspondence between theme and structure considered as parts of an aesthetic creation rather than as a necessity of logical discourse. Examples of the other kind of dialogue are numerous—Plato and Fontenelle, for instance. The subject of Plato's *Republic* is justice. Although the argumentation is intellectually exciting and leads in a variety of directions, one cannot speak of its having an aesthetic dimension in the work itself, of its being embedded in an aesthetic form peculiarly appropriate to it, rather than to some other subject. Two other factors contribute to Diderot's superiority in the aesthetics of the dialogue. The antagonists are not intellectual abstractions and effusions. Because their self-expression involves the fullness of life, and not only their opinions on a given subject, they are recognizable as personalities. Moreover, they are equally matched. There is no great teacher who inevitably and rather easily overmasters the opposition, pointing the way to a definitive solution. Indeed no answers are proposed. The work is a moral and aesthetic experiment, one which disturbs complacency at every moment and leads to no restful conclusion. That is the nature of the subject. Diderot's probing intellectual honesty will allow nothing but a clear look at it.

A second consideration worthy of emphasis pertains to the previously stated point, that the antagonists in the dialogue are engaged in the debate as total personalities. The psychological dimension is as inseparable from the argumentation as is the aesthetic. In fact, one may even venture to say that the specific arguments are scarcely entities in themselves. Each one bears the stamp of character and individual experience.

If we look at the confrontation from this viewpoint, it is quite clear that "Moi" may be considered as a member of the "Establishment" whose smugness is disturbed by the uncompromising egoism and nihilism of his adversary. "Lui" is the alienated outsider. His pantomimes should be interpreted as masks and disguises in which he expresses his alienation.

I do not intend to discuss here the complex question, about which so much has been written, of the author's personal relationship to his two characters. It is enough to say that both are essentially aesthetic creations which alter and surpass their biographical identity with their real-life prototypes. Yet this much merits emphasis. The successful figures of the High Enlightenment, as Robert Darnton has shown,[19] were absorbed into the Establishment, even while they continued to pursue reform or, in Diderot's case, to indulge in the privacy of their study in the temptations of radical thought, of which the present work is an outstanding example. And while I shall also refrain from discussing the psychological peculiarities of "Lui," the failures and frustrations that have caused his alienation, we may say that he is the analogue of Professor Darnton's radicalized "Grub Street" failures, and that his personality is disordered and unstable.

Le Neveu de Rameau is a drama of identity. Lui does not know who he is or who he wants to be—perhaps who he can be. The play of pride and abjection, of greatness and self-abasement, hinging on the need to feel his worth, which in turn depends less on his opinion of himself than on his place in the world and the "look" of

[19] R. Darnton, "The High Enlightenment and the Low-Life of Literature in Pre-Revolutionary France," *Past and Present,* No. 51, May 1971, pp. 81-115.

others—a need that itself requires self-alienation and the loss of identity—all this constitutes a strange inner drama that Diderot has captured in the most subtle and aesthetically valid terms.[20] Lui's acute self-awareness, his perception that he is not wholly any of his roles, leads to his cynicism, nihilism, and self-alienation. The aesthetic triumph of *Le Neveu de Rameau* is Diderot's expression by pantomime of an alienation that—again, in aesthetic terms—cannot be manifested by speech alone.

Moi, on the other hand, is in secure possession of his identity. His personality and his life, antithetical to Lui's, are *ordered.* He has founded his inner stability on the acceptance of recognized values and on a role in which he has succeeded, to his own rather smug satisfaction, in winning the esteem of others. Nevertheless, he is increasingly shaken by Lui, whose uncompromising cynicism becomes more and more a danger for his security and his values. Lui is a force, the disintegrating force, against which Moi must fight in order to safeguard the order and stability of his whole personality structure.

From a quite different and even opposing viewpoint, it is possible to argue that Lui disturbs Moi because Moi's conformism alienates him from an authentic self of which he is not aware, from a true liberation from the bondage of socially imposed moral categories. Moral acquiescence is, in a way, a surrender of the self (a theme Gide was to develop and one not unknown to the eighteenth century). Moi's inauthenticity is visible

[20] The inner drama is visible throughout, in changing modes. See, for example, pp. 46, 50, 52, 103. "The mask! The mask! I'd give one of my fingers to have found the mask." (All references to *Le Neveu de Rameau* are to Jean Fabre's critical edition, Genève, 1950.)

in his initial phrase, "My ideas are my whores." Intellectual "debauchery" provides him a false outlet, the illusion of freeing himself from the social code, without danger. Moi falls as far short of greatness, despite his talents, as Lui. Both are the objects of Diderot's satire.[21]

Since neither interlocutor is doctrinaire, they find themselves in agreement on many points; frequently Lui wins the more or less grudging assent of Moi. This complexity and crossing of lines adds to the truth of the characters and of the debate. As they prod each other, their personal engagement increases. The very character of Lui, his whole way of life as Diderot describes them in the interspersed fragments of autobiography, incarnate the principle of disorder. "He is a composite of arrogance and baseness, of common sense and derisiveness."[22] The notions of the proper and improper are "strangely scrambled in his head." His appearance, his habits, his dress, are a similar disharmony. The work's epigraph, referring to capriciously changing winds, describes him. Moi, who lives in a congealed state of conventionality, is fascinated by him (though he declares he cannot esteem him) because, he claims, such

[21] Ronald Grimsley points out that Diderot not infrequently defined a man's reality "not as a function of his submission to the rules of universal morality but as a function of a 'unity of character' that carries him beyond good and evil." Some men, instead of seeking self-realization, "lead a contradictory existence without being able to harmonize the discordant elements of their character." These contrast with Mme. de la Pommeraye, the Juif d'Avignon, Père Hudson, "who have achieved true unity of character and succeeded in winning a freedom which is uniquely theirs." Grimsley also suggests that Diderot himself finds a liberation in his novelistic world. ("L'ambigüité dans l'oeuvre romanesque de Diderot," *Cahiers de l'Association internationale des études françaises*, No. 13, Paris, 1961, pp. 225, 229, 236, 237.)

[22] Ibid., p. 4.

characters break the boring uniformity of respectable lives. The clash, when they meet, is instantaneous.

It begins with an apparent reversal of roles, as Moi defends the genius who disturbs the conventional order and tramples on moral values. But we soon see that Lui's opposition to such exceptionality rests in part on his preference for money and reckless sensual satisfactions. This leads immediately to the question of order in its widest cosmic dimension. Why hasn't nature established a better order, asks Lui, uniting greatness and goodness? For Moi, such an anthropomorphic complaint only upsets the "general order," which must be accepted as it is. Lui agrees, but from a quite different viewpoint. As long as he exists, "let all the rest go as it may."[23] The most perfect world, without him, can go to the devil. We may add, as he in effect does later, that as long as he is well off, the general order can go to the devil. The essence of his viewpoint is the accusation and the acceptance of man as an element of disorder. Man, who alone has awareness of order and disorder, orders everything in relation to himself. One might object that all animals do as much. However, in so doing, the animal, lacking such an awareness, remains a part of the natural order. The essence of Moi's attitude, as it will develop, is that this is not the case with man, inasmuch as he has invented a social and moral order. Ignoring its obligations creates disorder.

Lui's first pantomime, at this point, expresses the fantasy of the world recognizing his importance. While, like Jean Genêt in a later time, he takes pride in his debasement and seeks to create an authentic self through it, he longs for self-approbation and its confirmation in

[23] Ibid., p. 14.

the approbation of others. Authenticity thus becomes impossible. He will be a failure and will not achieve greatness. He does not want to despise himself or to be despised. To be great is his obsession: the phrase "grand homme" is repeated five times toward the end of the pantomime. His chosen métier, through which he aims at his goal, is that of parasite, buffoon, pimp. His métier is to live by his bad qualities, those which, paradoxically, allow others the ego-satisfying pleasure of despising him, and which could satisfy his aim only if they had the consistency and greatness his contrary needs make impossible. The second, brief pantomime is the counterpart of the first; in it he enacts symbolically his self-abasement and self-hatred. "And then, to despise oneself," he adds, "is unbearable."[24]

From the social viewpoint, his choice of life both expresses and foments disorder. But the former is more important. If seduction for pay adds to disorder, no one is seduced who does not want to be. Sexual drives and social commands are irreconcilable. An equally fundamental disorder is the inequity in the distribution of wealth and the good things of life, for it is without relation to talent, virtue, or merit. Everyone gets ahead as best he can, and always at the expense of others. This success, Lui realizes, is the only talent, the only virtue or merit that counts.[25] For Moi, his antagonist's view is perversity. Yet he admits to being perturbed:

[24] Ibid., p. 22.

[25] In *Satire I* (1773), Diderot exclaims: "How many different songs, how many discordant cries just in that forest called 'society.'" While he does not here mean the word "forêt" pejoratively, the image is revealing, and he goes on to give "mots de caractère" expressing human egoism and the law of the strong. (Donal O'Gorman, *Diderot the Satirist*, Toronto, 1971, p. 228.)

> Twenty times a burst of laughter prevents my anger from breaking forth; twenty times the anger that rose in my breast ended by a burst of laughter. I was disconcerted by so much wisdom and so much vileness; by ideas alternately so true and so false; by so general a perversity of feelings, so complete a corruption, and such uncommon frankness. He perceived the conflict that was going on inside of me.[26]

The word "perversity" implies an order of values. But what is the validity of that order, both in terms of its reality and of its real worth? Moi's efforts to establish them are surely less than convincing. "I think," Lui says at one point, "that not to have always enough to eat does not indicate a good order of things."[27] In fact, there is no order at all. "Nothing stable in this world. Today at the top of the wheel, tomorrow at the bottom. We are led by accursed circumstances; and they lead us very badly."[28] There is only one realistic position: in the world as it is, to live at the expense of others is not perversity, but nature's law of self-protection.[29] Moi cannot justify his judgment, and he is hampered by the fact that he is the *philosophe* who has "made it."

Death, as it always does, lies at the heart of the feeling of the absurd that Lui incarnates. He finds it in the fact that only in death are all equal. The revenge of merit comes too late. "The dead man does not hear the bells."

[26] *Le Neveu de Rameau*, p. 24.

[27] Ibid., p. 103.

[28] Ibid., pp. 102-103.

[29] According to James Doolittle, the "pantomime des gueux" (or of the "positions de Noverre") shows that for Lui all action is pantomime, or a fraud. "What is true for society is false for the individual, and vice versa. Truth is falsehood." (*Rameau's Nephew. A Study of Diderot's "Second Satire,"* Geneva, 1960, p. 51.) Implicit again is the notion of contradictory truths.

Indirectly, this fact justifies to him whatever one does in life. At this point he gives a wild, imaginary performance on a violin, followed by a fifth pantomime on the harpsichord. But the talent, in its fantastic exaggeration, is sham. Nor is it necessary, in society, really to have it, as the famous music lesson demonstrates.

Lui's picture of the world is developed steadily. Domination and exploitation rule the relations among men. Education is conceived accordingly, all other knowledge being frivolous. Morality consists of socially imposed conventions, accepted as such and nothing more, conventions which everyone violates as much as he can or dares to, in his own self-interest. The "idioms," as he calls the exceptions from the "general grammar" that each of us makes for himself (and for each there is only himself), are the symbols of nihilism and disorder. They characterize social life. Rousseau was to stand up against this situation and propose a way to invert it. The esteem and power which for Lui constitute the sole values are functions of this idiomatic success. "He who has a golden belt does not lack for fame. . . . In nature, all species devour each other, all ranks devour each other in society."[30] Class war is thus affirmed and nature's disorder (or an order composed of disorder) confirmed. In pre-Sadian fashion, the victim who is exploited is declared to have his just deserts. The basic biological drives are reasserted in all their primacy over the attempts of culture to order them.

Moi's sarcasm and supercilious mockery do not disturb his degraded opponent. He knows that he at least has the virtue of honesty. And he continues exposing

[30] *Le Neveu de Rameau*, p. 37. Happiness depends on instinctual satisfaction. "Men praise virtue, but they hate it and fly from it" (p. 44).

the hollowness under the masks of the various virtues. Gratitude, he says, more like Sade than La Rochefoucauld, is a burden, "and every burden is made to be shaken off."[31] Moi accepts the burden of virtue, as superior in *quality* to sensual pleasures, whose attractions are not to be denied. He falls back on that great myth of the times, the materialists' main hope for reconciling their philosophy with their moralism: only virtue brings happiness, and the wicked man is always unhappy, deep down. Lui denies both suppositions. The only remorse is for missed opportunities.[32] In sum, Lui's share in the dialogue amounts to a process of destruction of the norms by which society strives to order itself—the very framework of values and of civilization.

Not only are the norms factitious, they are fictitious. Only a few odd creatures are not hypocritical about them. The sentence, "It is the feeling and the language of all of society," forms a transition.[33] Now Lui will paint a vivid portrait of the Bertin menagerie, a microcosm of the social jungle, where *méchanceté* motivates

[31] Ibid., p. 40.

[32] R. Mauzi has shown that Diderot did not really believe in the virtue-happiness equivalence. He describes the role of Moi in these words: "Diderot seems to admit here, as a *philosophe,* an idea for which he will make Rameau's nephew responsible, the *philosophe's* responsibility at that moment being not to contradict him, for at bottom he agrees, but to oppose him with the equivocal resistance of an epicureanism broad enough to embrace both the voluptuousness of a good conscience and sensual pleasures. He seems ready to believe that to be happy is to be oneself; that is, to preserve the truth which is peculiar to our being, and which may choose to express itself through a passion incompatible with virtue." ("Diderot et le bonheur," *Diderot Studies III,* Genève, 1961, pp. 265-66.) For Diderot's scorn for mediocrity, see passages quoted by Mauzi, ibid., p. 279.

[33] *Le Neveu de Rameau,* p. 55.

men and women. The portrait is designed to uncover the real disorder underneath the appearance or illusion of a social order. "Wolves are not hungrier; tigers are not more cruel." In the subtle and deep paradox in which Lui plays on the word "fou" in its double meaning of "jester" and "mad,"[34] he epitomizes human relationships as a play of power, pride, superiority, exploitation—a theme so important to eighteenth-century ethics that to ignore it is to distort almost everything.[35] In an epigram, he touches a fundamental problem of eighteenth-century speculation, which the conventional moralist, Moi, cannot overcome: "we must be what self-interest requires us to be." This is the one universal law of behavior. It leads to another great theme of the dialogue: everyone plays roles, and everyone must play his own. "Palissot has done his duty." The wolves and hyenas of the world have their roles. The strong must devour the weak, and the victim gets no tears. "All that is set down in the tacit pact. It's just too bad for anyone who doesn't know it or forgets it."[36] The pact justifies the wicked. We even admire them, and they are entitled to our admiration, when they display integrity of character and reach heights of greatness. To celebrate the triumph of the evil renegade, and of all men great in evil, Lui enters into his sixth pantomime, a song in the form of a fugue.

We must pass over the aesthetic self-expression of Lui, in musical theory and practice,[37] even as we cannot here study the intricacies of the psychological relationships between Lui and Moi. The two are not unrelated.

[34] Ibid., p. 61.

[35] See L. G. Crocker, *An Age of Crisis*, ch. 11.

[36] *Le Neveu de Rameau*, p. 69.

[37] See Doolittle, *op. cit.*, pp. 48-51.

Moreover, the themes of art and morality are fused in the third and final section of the dialogue, when Moi tries to propose the Shaftesburian notion of a relation between beauty and virtue. Lui's reply is summarized in the repeated idea that wealth and power are all. "If he has a lot of gold he will lack nothing, not even your esteem."[38] The theme of disorder now reaches once again beyond the social life of man to cosmic dimensions. "Everything that lives, and men are no exception, seeks its own good at the expense of whoever it may be."[39] It is the work of culture, of "education," to put a brake on aggressiveness, to prevent the sexually aroused youth from killing his father and copulating with his mother. Lui admits this, but adds that a good upbringing is one that teaches how to indulge one's aggressivity without danger. His own life, with its failure to achieve greatness, its lack of integrity, its ups and downs, is brought forward as an illustration of disorder in the world.

Lui is not one to hover at the cosmic level. "I am in this world and I stay in it"—a statement which in the mouth of Moi would be a humanistic *profession de foi.* To Lui it is a matter of appetite, and literally, of hunger. Echoing what Diderot had perhaps written or suggested at the end of Rousseau's second *Discours,* he protests against that fundamental disorder which is injustice. "What a devil of an economy, with some men who have a surfeit of everything, while others have a stomach as importunate as they, and nothing to put under their teeth." It is this fact, this declaration, that leads to the famous pantomime of the positions, a pantomime that portrays with nihilistic mockery the game of life—hid-

[38] *Le Neveu de Rameau,* p. 93.

[39] Ibid., p. 95.

eous, mad, but most of all absurd. In his recognition of the absurdity of the world, Lui expresses his role as the stranger, an alienation incarnated in this tenth pantomime. Each of us has his role, or position, in the dance—Moi is swept away into this key admission. "Whoever needs another is indigent and takes a pose. . . . Yes, indeed, what you call the beggars' pantomime is what keeps the world spinning."[40] Was not Jean-Jacques Rousseau's revolt precisely against this? His dream was one of a world in which the indignities of *dependence* would be eliminated. He, too, was a stranger, a *gueux*, and had played many positions in the dance.

The next two pantomimes continue and cap with their virtuosity the fundamental display of the tenth. As Lui apes the hypocritical, flattering abbé and the sexy strutting of his own wife, we achieve the deepest realization of the alienation that comes from his awareness of the game of life others play without realizing it; while his awareness of the disorder and absurdity of the world illuminates his willed degradation—precisely as we see it in our own time, in Jean Genêt. Values? There is only life. He has the final word: "Rira bien qui rira le dernier."

We have seen that while the debate between Lui and Moi seems to be asking whether the human will is good or evil, an underlying and unexpressed question is whether it is authentic or alienated. According to Lionel Trilling, we must ask whether the true self is the "best self" or something that is more authentic because it violates the social standard of the "best self." Proust encapsulated this idea in his own beautiful way in *La Fugitive*: "each of us is not one person, but contains several persons who do not all have the same moral

[40] Ibid., p. 105.

value." Diderot's penetration has a different scope. It emphasizes the self's exposure to the "look" of others, its unavoidable response to their demand that we display our self for its judgment, and the resulting absorption of the self into the roles it must play to meet that demand—an idea symbolically expressed with the full force of Diderot's genius in the histrionics of the "positions."[41]

From the black humor of *Le Neveu de Rameau* to the light-hearted gaiety of *Jacques le Fataliste* (1773) is a leap forward in more than one way; but the underlying world picture is, beneath the altered tonalities, the same. The outstanding change is aesthetic. We must reiterate that all of Diderot's novels and tales are simultaneously aesthetic and moral experiments. In *Le Neveu de Rameau* we have an artfully concealed order underlying

[41] Here again Trilling's remarks about sincerity in relation to society are most perceptive. He underlines the necessity of considering three factors: the person judging, the correspondence between the principles avowed by a society and its actual conduct, the extent to which a society fosters or corrupts the sincerity of its citizens. "The last of these considerations is the subject of a work which must always have a special place in the development of the ideal of sincerity, *Le Neveu de Rameau.*" It would be more accurate to say that all three considerations are involved in the *Neveu.* Trilling's interpretation is similar to my own. Lui's "thwarted passion for what society has to offer goes along with a scornful nihilism which overwhelms every prudential consideration." Stronger than desire for respect is his appetite for demonstrative self-abasement: "his ego, betraying its proper function, turns on itself and finds expression in compulsive buffoonery, at once inviting shame and achieving shamelessness in a fashion that Dostoevski was to make familiar." Mimetic skill is "the essence of his being." (*Sincerity and Authenticity,* New York, 1973, pp. 27-32. Cf. my own article, "*Le Neveu de Rameau,* une expérience morale.")

the appearance of reckless confusion. The aesthetic impression contributes to the conceptual meanings of the dialogue; they are, one may say, embedded in that impression. A drastic change takes place in *Jacques le Fataliste.* The author now displays himself to the reader in the act of deliberately creating confusion—and in the very process of writing his novel. Even more, he makes the reader his accomplice, by discussing it, with apparent jocularity, with him. The usual abolition of aesthetic distance between the reader and the book he is reading is thereby reversed. The reader is no longer contemplating a fictitious real world (somewhat analogous to the three walls of the realistic theater); he is associated with the author, at such moments, more than with the characters of the story. At the same time, the author is inventing himself, as he distantiates himself from the creative act.

The willful arbitrariness Diderot the *poetas* or demiurge flaunts before his readers, playing with them like a wanton boy, does more than place in question the validity of Jacques' naive fatalism and the existential validity of determinism, perhaps irrefutable as logic, on which Jacques also expatiates, neglecting to distinguish the two. It mirrors a capricious world, of gods or of men, and almost approaches the doctrine of "freedom of indifference" that from early in the century had been the focus of the determinists' attack on free will.

In Diderot's novel, in both the dialogue and the commentary, there is a repeated interplay of chance versus fatalism. Jacques claims that the former is a semblance explained by the latter. Either one excludes, from the standpoint of subjective cognition, the predictable cause-effect regularity of eighteenth-century scientific materialism, and of Diderot's own world view. The arbitrary, almost foreshadowing the "absurd" of a later day, flies, so to speak, at the book's masthead.

There is no need for us to go into detail on this matter. Various critics have brought out the arbitrariness of incidents, and Diderot's insistent commentary can escape no reader of the novel.[42] A remark of Jacques' speaks for itself, in regard to the ultimate significance involved:

> The fact is that, for lack of knowing what is written up there, we know neither what we want nor what we do, and we follow our fantasy which we call reason, or our reason which is often only a dangerous fantasy that sometimes turns out well and sometimes bad.[43]

We cannot, he goes on, foresee the results of our acts. "Is it we who lead destiny, or destiny that leads us? How many projects, wisely planned, have come to nought . . . ! How many madcap projects have succeeded . . . !" Could this truth be brought home more dramatically than in the episode of the story of Mme. de la Pommeraye? An extravagant project succeeds, but with effects contrary to the plotter's calculations. Existentially, this is the triumph of chance. The outcome, typical of human relations, defies justification in terms of causal law. Such a world in which we, like Jacques and his master, stumble along blindly, announces the absurd. The opening line of the novel reads: "How had they met? By chance, like everyone else." And its refrain is "Do we know where we are going?" The chaos of

[42] The major statement remains J. Robert Loy's *Diderot's Determined Fatalist*, New York, 1950.

[43] Diderot, *Oeuvres romanesques*, ed. Henri Bénac, Paris, 1962, p. 503.

events is expressed by Jacques when he recounts to his master what has happened during a brief separation.

> Listen carefully. I went, I fought, I stirred up all the peasants in the countryside, I stirred up all the city dwellers, I was taken for a highwayman, I was led to the judge, I underwent two interrogations, I almost had two men hanged; I had a valet dismissed, I had a servant girl sacked, I was convicted of having gone to bed with a wench I never saw and whom I nonetheless paid; and I came back.[44]

Later he says, "Good brings ill, ill brings good. We walk in the night beneath what is written up there, equally mad in our wishes, in our joy and in our affliction."[45] But Jacques goes further than an affirmation of human blindness. "One never knows what Heaven wants or doesn't want, and perhaps Heaven itself doesn't know either."[46] The universe, without plan or order, may be a madhouse.

Can the human world help reflecting cosmic disorder? The moral world of man, we see in *Jacques le Fataliste*, is equally chaotic and absurd. Le Pelletier, the good man, is publicly rewarded with a slap. Jacques is capable of altruism, and is victimized for it, leading the master to a remark reminiscent of Zadig's cosmic protest.[47] Gousse is equally capable of vile and heroic actions.

[44] See ibid., p. 521. Also p. 655: "Well, my master! who knows what is written up there? Let anyone say now that it is good or bad to give one's money; that it is a misfortune to be knocked out. Without those two events, M. Desglands would never have heard of Jacques."

[45] Ibid., p. 573.

[46] Ibid., p. 586.

[47] Ibid., p. 572. Jacques will later make a similar remark (p. 655).

Friendship and jealousy cohabit in the master's heart. Our ideas and our acts may be contradictory.

The chaos of human life is centered, in Diderot's picture, on three factors: sex, moral judgment, and the drive toward power, superiority, and exploitation of others. The sexual instincts are an irreducible element of disorder in society. Rousseau, recognizing the same fact, sought ways of overcoming it by various means of control; Diderot accepts it as inevitable. The sentimental elements of love, its declarations of uniqueness and fidelity, are illusions. The law of flux makes of romantic "eternal love" a vain human ideal or longing. Diderot expresses these ideas poetically, then goes at once to the fable of the sheath and the knife to indicate the futility of social restrictions.[48]

Here, as in the *Supplément au Voyage de Bougainville*, *Le Rêve de d'Alembert*, and in various other places, Diderot, like Buffon, reduces love to its physical aspects. It appears, in such contexts, as an organic appetite or instinct. Again, the emotional accompaniments are not consistently denied, but they are at best evanescent illusions (the Vieillard's "biens imaginaires"), accessories of physical experience, subservient to its shifting whims. Diderot will define love as the voluptuous friction of two membranes, or the voluptuous loss of a few drops of fluid. The chapter on the passions in *Eléments de physiologie* describes them in physical terms.

Disorder results, then, in two different ways. Having implicitly distinguished sex from love in the *Supplément au Voyage de Bougainville*, Diderot seems to consider sex as disorderly from a purely rational viewpoint, but not as intrinsically productive of social or moral

[48] Ibid., p. 605.

disorder. Quite to the contrary, it is when men try to *introduce* order into this anodyne natural disorder, that real disorder ensues. The sage native of Tahiti, Orou, immediately guesses that there is a great deal of adultery under the "civilized" marriage system.[49] Other forms of repression create pathological disorder in the individual. These physiological and psychological phenomena are described by Diderot in *Le Rêve de d'Alembert* ("Suite de l'entretien"[50]) and in the vivid scenes of *La Religieuse.* Contrasting with Mme. de la Carlière's fierce possessiveness is Jacques' naïve and healthy expression of his instincts; his Rabelaisian joy creates no harm or disorder, only mutual pleasures.[51] The antagonism between the sexes is that of two partners in a game in which neither is hurt.

The second source of disorder lies in the human dimensions men have added to the pleasure of physical sexual activity. If sex is chaotic, love makes it worse. In the mature and wiser perspectives of the *Réfutation d'Helvétius,* Diderot not only admits a purely psychological dimension of love, but insists on it as the phenomenon which distinguishes human sexuality from that of other animals.

> You who attribute so much power to the impulsion of one sex toward the other, consider that a vigorous

[49] See the entire third and fourth sections of the *Supplément* and particularly the statement, "the passion of love, reduced to a simple physical appetite, produced none of our disorders there" (*Oeuvres philosophiques,* pp. 503-504).

[50] *Oeuvres philosophiques,* pp. 276-79.

[51] Jacques' Rabelaisian joy is precisely what Diderot prescribes in his *Entretiens avec Catherine II* and his *Observations sur le Nakaz,* though his tone there is closer to that of Lui. See Diderot, *Oeuvres politiques,* ed. P. Vernière, Paris, 1963, pp. 295-96, 411-12.

> but unfeeling man will be drawn by his passion toward a woman only as a bull is drawn to the heifer; he is the wild beast of Lucretius who, his sides pierced by a mortal arrow, throws himself upon the hunter and covers him with his blood. He will scarcely compose elegies or madrigals.
>
> He wants to satisfy himself, and is not concerned with touching or pleasing. A burning, abundant and acrid fluid irritates his organs of pleasure. Such a one does not sigh, he roars; he does not turn tender and languishing eyes and moist eyelids upon the object of his passion; his eyes are flashing and his look devours her. Like the stag in autumn, he lowers his horns and drives the timid doe before him. In the corner of the dark forest where he has directed her, he busies himself intensely with securing his happiness, without thinking of that of the creature he is submitting to him; satisfied, he leaves her and withdraws. Try, if you can, to make a tender and delicate poet out of that beast. He has only one word, or none at all.[52]

But alongside the poetry of love, there is the havoc wreaked by *le chagrin d'amour,* touchingly portrayed in devastating effects in Mlle. de la Chaux's despair and wretchedness, in *Ceci n'est pas un conte.* True love knows no limit to giving, even to an ungrateful "monster." This is one of the few occasions when we find Diderot interested in love as a romantic phenomenon, in its full human dimension. We are made to see that real love exposes us to unhappy, destructive consequences. Mlle. de la Chaux's lover. Gardeil, has only physical pleasure, and is immune to all the rest. Who is the real "monster," the unviable being—the pleasure-seeker or

[52] *Oeuvres philosophiques*, p. 587.

love's victim? The further reach of love's damage is not, however, caused by love itself, but by its entanglement with other sensitive areas of the ego, especially pride and self-esteem, and the consequent mutability of love into resentment, even hatred. In Mme. de la Pommeraye we see this aspect of the trauma of *chagrin d'amour*, just as its other faces are revealed in *Mme. de la Carlière* and *Ceci n'est pas un conte*. Nowhere, however, does Diderot portray the ravages of jealousy.

Still, despite his occasional cynical, materialistic or primitivistic reductionism, Diderot has gone a long way in showing how love engages the self completely, in all its physical, emotional, and psychic dimensions. It creates a unique interrelationship. Perhaps it is not going too far to suggest that, if reciprocal, it creates a new kind of quasi-organic unity, an interpersonal structure subject, like other structures, to stresses and tensions, to eventual deterioration or disintegration, and most damaging of all, to explosive disruption, somewhat analogous to natural catastrophe.

In *Jacques le Fataliste*, at all events, we are made to see that sexual energy is only one configuration of a larger, universal pattern of disorder (to use a rather contradictory phrase). The psychological, or specifically human, aspect of sex and the work of culture are submitted to the overriding anarchism of natural drives. The true character of the relationship between the sexes is portrayed as exploitation, willed or unconscious, by the stronger or more clever of the two. The stories of Gousse, his wife and his mistress, of the pastry cook and the intendant, of the surgeon, of Mme. de la Pommeraye and the Marquis des Arcis; the incidental bawdy episodes, Father Hudson's seraglio, and the nefarious doings of the Chevalier de Saint-Ouin, all testify to the same truth. All take life in society to be a form of warfare, in which the strong lives by victimizing the weak, for the sake of pleasure, power, superiority, or just survival. This picture is the common one in the eighteenth-century novel. Lovers, friends, parents, and children—all are and always will be each other's dupes.[53] The "other" is reduced to the status of an object, or a means, and thus deprived of human status as an end in itself. Nowhere is this more evident than in Mme. de la Pommeraye's complete submission to her ends of the two women she uses as instruments. The parable of the dogs, which expresses Diderot's view, is only a new version of the pantomime of the "positions de Noverre" in *Le Neveu de Rameau.*

> Jacques asked his master whether he had not noticed that no matter how impoverished the common people were, they all had dogs. . . . Whence he concluded that every man wanted to command another. . . . Well! said Jacques, everyone has his dog. The minister is the king's dog, the first clerk is the minister's dog, the wife is her husband's dog, or the husband his wife's . . . weak men are the dogs of the strong.[54]

Not content with the parable, Diderot had already expressed the same idea twice before in this novel.[55] The lesson is clearly drawn, in action and in precept. As the Hostess says, the dog does not hurt you, while the others do.[56]

Diderot is not enraged by the spectacle, as Voltaire is in *Candide,* or Rousseau in the *Préface de Narcisse.* In a universe in which necessary laws eventuate in con-

[53] *Oeuvres romanesques,* p. 701.

[54] Ibid., pp. 667-68.

[55] Ibid., pp. 537, 563.

[56] Ibid., p. 596. This idea is also used by Camus, in *La Chute.*

tingency, blind chance, and the absence of moral ground or justification, the human struggle to create order is waged against overwhelming odds. The idea of chance, "le hasard," opens and closes the novel, and recurs again and again. We can grasp the reach of Jacques' speculation:

> How many strange things are written up there! There is a child on the way, God knows how! Who knows the role the little bastard will play in the world? Who knows whether he wasn't born for the happiness or the destruction of an empire? . . . Why shouldn't a Cromwell come from a turner's shop?[57]

Diderot may have felt, like Voltaire, that for men to live this way is to compound the cosmic scandal of waste, irrationality, and the absurd, and to connive in it. In the works we have considered, however, he is closer to Marivaux's attitude of the detached spectator, or investigator, than to Voltaire's intense moral concern. This attitude is translated into Diderot's clearly expressed admiration for the "sublime rascal."[58] Pettiness and failure are the sins in *Jacques le Fataliste* as in several other writings of Diderot, whether they are expressed in virtue or in vice. Greatness of character is always, *malgré nous,* admirable. "More villainous actions are done every day, without any genius. You can hate, you can fear Mme. de la Pommeraye; you will not despise her."[59] The losers receive short shrift from life, or from Diderot's own sympathies.

It has more than once been pointed out that Diderot stresses the uncertainties if not the impossibilities of moral judgment in *Jacques le Fataliste,*[60] as he does in

[57] Ibid., p. 768. [58] Ibid., p. 684. [59] Ibid., p. 651.
[60] Ibid., pp. 544, 562.

other tales and dialogues. This psychological obstacle, apparently as radical as the absence of a ground for morals in the alien world of nature outside of man himself, adds further elements to the portrayal of disorder, further difficulties to the search for order that characterizes the thought of the Enlightenment, and is perhaps its central problem. The *philosophes* realized that we are destined to struggle with and within the antithesis of nature and culture. Although they sometimes made that antithesis more absolute than it really is, they also realized the interpenetration of the two elements. Man is a part of the commonality of nature. Jacques' remark about mosquitos is pure moral nihilism: "They are thinking of themselves; and everything in nature thinks of itself and thinks only of itself. What matter if it hurts others, as long as it's good for us."[61] The statement is one possible logical consequence of Diderot's "affirmation of a metaphysical flux which would imply a correlative ethical flux."[62] However, it is not a necessary consequence, or one we can accept with tranquillity, unless one denies (as he occasionally seems to do), the legitimacy and primacy of cultural value over natural or instinctual value. Diderot knows that our nature also makes us creatures of culture.

Culture is the creation of a human order that cannot exist without the acceptance of moral values. "I define virtue, the taste for order in moral things. The taste for order, in general, dominates us from earliest child-

[61] Ibid., p. 756.

[62] S. L. Kabelac, *op. cit.*, p. 99. Cf. the statement in a letter to Mme. de Maux (?): "Everything is equivalent for [nature]. The good man and the wicked are indistinguishable in the universal arrangement of things" (*Correspondance*, vol. IX, 179).

hood."[63] Diderot most often maintains that society has its legitimate demands, though his view of their relation to individual demands varies considerably. Obligation inheres in man's rational nature and in his needs as a social creature who is dependent for his happiness on his relations with others in a community. In his published writings, Diderot makes happiness a function of virtue or altruism (and this is also Moi's position in *Le Neveu de Rameau*). At other times overriding importance is attributed to ego-satisfaction, as a value or at least as a fact of life.

Culture must contend with the anarchic canker that nature has planted within us. Rousseau, with his clear recognition of this human duplicity, dreamed of eliminating the poisonous *moi humain* in a new kind of society composed of men remade. Diderot had no such dream. Without the millennium and the utopia, he saw mankind condemned to re-enact perpetually the struggle for order against unconquerable disorder. The conflict is ever-present, in life and in his own mind. Its extension leads us into the realm of politics, where we shall again see that human life, in its own way, mirrors the great law of universal process.

[63] *Entretiens sur le Fils naturel*, in *Oeuvres esthétiques*, p. 128. Diderot repeats this idea more than once. Speaking of remorse and conscience in his commentary on Hemsterhuis, he writes: "We cannot long exist without conceiving ideas of order and disorder, of good actions and bad." We project on our own actions the judgments we would make of the same actions of other men. (*Commentaire sur la "Lettre sur l'homme et ses rapports,"* p. 71.)

IV.
Politics

POLITICS BY ITS NATURE DEALS WITH the question of disorder and order, since government exists in good part to overcome the one and to foster the other. Diderot is keenly aware of this central problem, and is particularly mindful of its relation to the liberty of individuals.

Diderot's political thought underwent a dramatic evolution—perhaps one should say, in some ways, a revolution—in the early 1770's.[1] In the *Encyclopédie,* his views are rather conventional and, even when they exceed the bounds of prudence, as in "Autorité politique" (1751), evolve entirely in the sphere of abstractions, as was indeed typical of the Holbachian circle.[2] In the later period, he undergoes the influence of Galiani's realism and of his own contacts with real situations in the Langres region, in Russia, and in Holland. It is then that he takes a more radical turn, and a more empirical one, although he never escapes the mold of abstract rationalism.

Eighteenth-century writers, often accused of being

[1] See Paul Vernière's excellent introduction to Diderot, *Oeuvres politiques,* Paris, Garnier, 1963. Page references, unless otherwise noted, will be to this volume.

[2] How much of "Autorité politique" represents Diderot's own thought is presently uncertain. See J. Lough, *Essays on the "Encyclopédie" of Diderot and d'Alembert,* London, 1968, chapter VII.

ahistorical (and they were in some ways), were operating within a framework in which historical genesis was in fact a prominent element. Genetic speculations, though they often pretended and intended to be empirical, were largely rationalistic and imaginary. The origin of society was one of the most popular of those abstract questions which exercised such a fascination over the men of that time. It was related to the legitimacy of a society, and ultimately to the order or disorder it implied. The *Encyclopédie*, for instance, returns to it frequently. The theory of a natural gregarious instinct vied with the contractual theory, which had several variations, while the idea of a gradual extension of the natural unit of family also had considerable appeal. While many held to the vision of the weak uniting for protection against the strong, Rousseau, standing as he so often did alone, had proposed the novel idea, typical of his mentality, of a conspiracy of the strong against the weak.

On this question, Diderot's opinions reveal an interesting development. "Autorité politique" does not deal directly with it; but the subject of the article—the nature of a legitimate society—implies the question, and he attempts to answer it. The submission involved in a social organization is not natural, he declares. Paternal authority, which is natural, ends in the state of nature with the independence of adulthood. Legitimate authority derives then from an implicit or an actual contract.[3]

Diderot's analysis of the conditions of a legitimate contract do not concern us. We need only retain two central ideas. Human will and rationality preside over

[3] In the *Apologie de l'abbé de Prades*, Diderot attributes the origin of society to the mutuality of needs. Government and laws then come into being to prevent the anarchy arising from nature's law of the strong. (*Oeuvres complètes*, I, 455, 465-66.)

the formation and the form of a legitimate society; in this regard, at least, the fundamental perspective is not different from Rousseau's. Diderot's concrete analysis of legitimacy suggests that the political institutions of most societies, including the French, violate these conditions. Paradoxically, it follows that we must dismiss "Autorité politique" as a historical or genetic account. Most societies are organized in a way that controvenes what the article sets forth as the abstract conditions of legitimacy, and these are not seen in any connection with even a hypothetical account of how societies came into being. What Diderot describes is what should be, not what is or what has been. He admits that such abstract notions arise only at a much later stage. Nonetheless there remains the puissant implication that order cannot exist in a polity which embodies the forceful violation of the rational principles of order, and that the actual history of societies has been such a consistent violation. A further implication, to be developed in later writings, is that the thrust toward social order is related to conceptual or rational orderings, and needs, while actual behavior responds to more elementary, deep-seated motives and drives. Thus the antithesis is recreated at the political level.

In his later period, Diderot retains many of the ideas of "Autorité politique," but puts them into a significantly different setting. In one of his papers written for Catherine (*Entretiens avec Catherine II*, 1773), it becomes clear that all societies are disorderly in their inception, in their normal evolutionary course, and in their functioning. Now he mocks speculations on the origin of society: "a fine text for that species of birds who fatten on fog and who are called metaphysicians."[4]

[4] *Oeuvres politiques*, p. 303.

He discredits all three theories we have mentioned: gregarious instinct, family, a contract of the weak against the strong. (He does not mention Rousseau's theory of a conspiratorial plot of the strong against the weak.) Instead he suggests one of his own: the origin of society is in the ineluctable war of man against nature. Diderot's naturalism infiltrates his rationalism. Needs (a notion that long before had been made the central point in the genesis of moral ideas, in the *Apologie de l'abbé de Prades,* and the *Lettre sur les aveugles,* and to a certain extent, of aesthetic ideas, in "Du Beau"), a large part of which are also dangers, brought men into organized forms of living.

Unfortunately, nothing in this process is inherently order-promoting. Following Rousseau's critique in the *Discours sur l'origine de l'inégalité,* Diderot—and we know that he had played a small part in shaping its ideology—affirms that social living created a new enemy and new dangers: "reciprocal enmity between societies has followed the struggle with nature. Isolated man had only one adversary, nature. Man in society has two, man and nature."[5] Having said this, Diderot does not at once extend his idea to the broader reach of Rousseau's critique, the warfare among men within any given society. Instead he makes the state of warfare the attribute of tyranny. Any factor that breaks the social unity, that turns union into disunion, is disastrous: "every man works for himself and the state of savagery is reborn." The *grande maxime* of tyranny is "divide and rule." It wants the absurdity of "a society and isolated men." Diderot does not go on like Rousseau to seek a radical

[5] Ibid., p. 305. See note 3, above. The intended order of law never has worked as well as we should like it to, because man is *duplex.*

remedy in the theoretical construct of an organic or "true" society. He contents himself with the statement that whatever brings men together is good, whatever drives them away from "the true notion of society" is bad. It will become obvious in the sequel that Rousseau's idea of a "true society" would have had no appeal to Diderot.

It is as manifest in Diderot's later political writings as it is in such pieces as *Le Neveu de Rameau* and *Jacques le Fataliste* that he has no illusions about the character of human societies. In *Pages contre un tyran* (1771), he defends d'Holbach for having portrayed the world as it really is, "full of liars, crooks, oppressors of all sorts."[6] If the description lacks the compelling detail and picturesque eloquence of Rousseau, and its deep causative analysis, it is at least decisive. But he goes on, explaining why lies are triumphant: "there are so many enemies of the true, the good and the right; so many false laws; so many bad governments; so much immorality ('mauvaises moeurs'); so many men who find their self-interest in evil."

Diderot indirectly takes up the same theme again in the *Entretiens avec Catherine II* when he expounds on another abstract question that was perennial in the eighteenth century, luxury. His point is to establish a rather tenuous distinction between two kinds of luxury. First there is the bad kind, which results in vast inequality and the deification of money, the only power, the only source of consideration. Display, reckless emulation, dissimulation, and above all the unprincipled race for riches create a fundamental disorder in a society so oriented. Morals are ruined by "wealth, the mother of vices." The fine arts have been reduced to the "filth"

[6] Ibid., p. 136.

of Boucher. Even the mechanical arts are prostituted to fashion and display. Parents neglect the education of their children in order to live in style. Sons are forced to enter the church and daughters relegated to a cloister. "There are no more fathers, or mothers, or relatives, or friends. . . . The detailing of this corruption would never end."[7] Rousseau is still echoing loudly in our ears, with an overlay of Diderot's pet foes. It follows that the poor must draw blood from the rich:

> "Eh! let all these hungry insects that surround those bodies swollen with fat fasten on them, sting them, suck them and draw drop by drop a small portion of that blood they took by emptying the veins of their fellow-citizens."[8]

In the *Supplément au Voyage de Bougainville* (1772), echoes of Rousseau still sound strong: "Tell me whether, in any country at all, there lives a father who, were he not restrained by shame, would not rather lose his child, or a husband his wife, than his fortune and comfort for the rest of his life."[9]

This radical critique of money-centered, acquisitive, competitive societies leads Diderot to no revolutionary plan, to nothing like Rousseau's grand conception, but only to a demand for the reform of major abuses concerning taxes, priests, and privileges. Any reader of Rousseau will feel that the depths of the problem remain untouched. With historical hindsight, we know that such reforms do not dissipate disorder or create a "true society," and we are tempted again to accuse Diderot (as Catherine did) of a naïve rationalism typical

[7] Ibid., p. 288.
[8] Ibid., p. 286.
[9] *Oeuvres philosophiques*, p. 499. See also the satire of luxury inserted into the *Salon de 1767, Oeuvres complètes*, XI, 90-96.

of his time. All of this is true, but it is not the whole truth. We shall see that Diderot does not really believe his ideal goals to be realizable. He is willing to settle for something less, and he would surely not have purchased order at the price that Rousseau realistically said had to be paid.

The two ideas, that of the present state of society and that of possibilities for the future, are obviously related. In the *Observations sur le Nakaz* (1774), Diderot dropped the mask of prudence he had carefully maintained the year before. Now he ridicules as inadequate Catherine's statement that enlightenment ("les lumières") would reduce crime. "Make your subjects happy," he retorts. There are more crimes in Paris than in the forests. The truth is, then, that "a society that is not well ordered is worse than the savage state." He continues:

> The word "society" suggests a state of union, of peace, of the harmony of all individual wills in the furtherance of a common goal, the general happiness. The thing is exactly the contrary. It is a state of war; war of the sovereign against his subjects; war of the subjects against each other. . . .
>
> In the moral as in the physical realm, it is easier to go down than to go up again. A descending body follows its natural bent, and it is against its nature, by the effect of an accidental and violent shock, that it goes up for a brief moment.[10]

While in the first paragraph we see how Diderot is attracted by Rousseau's concepts, in the second he stops short at the point of the latter's pessimism about corrupted societies and is not interested in going beyond it

[10] *Oeuvres politiques*, p. 401.

and in fabricating the hypothetical structure of an ideal society. Like many others in his time, he was uninterested in Rousseau's *Contrat social*—even as Morelly's work went unnoticed. We do not know that he ever read it, even though he calls it unoriginal in the phillipic in the *Essai sur les règnes de Claude et de Néron*. If he did, he did not understand it, and I am inclined to favor the first alternative. In the *Réfutation d'Helvétius* (1775), his remarks on Rousseau refer only to the second *Discours* and embody the common misreading of that work: "If Rousseau, instead of sermonizing us to return to the woods, had undertaken to imagine a kind of society that would be half civilized and half savage, it would have been very difficult, I think, to answer him."[11] In Diderot's willingness, here and in the *Supplément au Voyage de Bougainville*, to entertain the possibility of halting the dynamics of cultural evolution, once unleashed, we see once again that he was less a realist than Rousseau, and a less profound thinker in the sphere of political philosophy.

We have observed Diderot's suggestion that the basic causes of social disorder lie in the failure of social structures to achieve a true unity that could cope with the egoistic and aggressive vitalities of the individual. He knows, as the *Supplément au Voyage de Bougainville* makes clear, that social life, though natural to the human species, involves the elaboration of artificial norms, patterns, and limits that contravene what he calls "natural man." To Bougainville's primitive, they are only "hindrances, disguised in a hundred different forms."[12] Of course Diderot is cheating, *pour la cause*, since the Tahitians, as Rousseau had cogently urged,

[11] Ibid., p. 472.
[12] *Oeuvres philosophiques*, p. 464.

were not in the state of nature, but had an advanced tribal organization with very many "hindrances." Diderot, however, had convinced himself that the Tahitians had stopped at the right point: "a people wise enough to have by themselves halted at a middle stage."[13]

Exactly like Rousseau, he sees man divided between irreconcilable demands. "Do you want an abridged history of almost all our unhappiness? Here it is. There existed a natural man; an artificial man was introduced into that man; and a continual war, throughout life, arose within the cavern."[14] This idea he emphasizes further in the *Salon de 1767*: "The fact is that the civil law and the religious law are in contradiction with the law of nature. What will be the result? Since all three will be alternately broken and observed, they will lose all punitive sanction. One is neither religious, nor a citizen, nor a man. One is only what the interest of the moment requires."[15] Unlike Rousseau, Diderot does not say: "Give him all to the State, or leave him all to himself."[16] He does not urge the statesman to teach man not to be in contradiction with himself, to suppress or sublimate the *moi humain* by a process that will outwit and reconstruct nature.[17] On the contrary, he seems to be answering Rousseau's "we must denature man," in *Emile*, when he cries: "The empire of nature cannot be destroyed; oppose whatever obstacles you will to it, it will persist. . . . Even if you become ruthless, you will not succeed in denaturing me."[18]

[13] Ibid., p. 503.

[14] Ibid., pp. 510-11.

[15] *Oeuvres complètes*, XI, 121. The same idea is repeated in *Pages contre un tyran*, p. 142.

[16] *The Political Writings of Jean Jacques Rousseau*, ed. C. E. Vaughan, Cambridge, 1915, vol. I, 326.

[17] Rousseau, "Economie politique," *passim*.

[18] *Oeuvres philosophiques*, p. 510.

The problem of disorder is rooted, then, in the ambiguity of human nature. Carl Becker would doubtless have considered the continued notion of *homo duplex* as a disguised prolongation of Christian modes of thought. The difference, however, outweighs the mere formalism of duality. What Diderot and others in the eighteenth century have in mind is not the neo-Platonic combination of bestial and divine, of body and spirit that for the Christian constitutes the human enigma. For these secularists the ambiguity lies in the coexistence of two empirically verifiable factors, a natural order and a social order. Both are purely human; at least, neither a remote animal origin nor a supposititious divine plan can be meaningfully considered, and they are discarded.

The "natural" in the problem has two parts. There is a basic biological component in the human element: survival, self-interest, the pleasure-pain motive as it was endlessly expounded. But the more important element is psychological. It is what I have called the "pride complex." The need for the feelings of superiority and prestige, and for power, require visible signs and confirmation. Exploitation, cruelty, and a so-called "state of war" ensue. Diderot, Helvétius, and many other writers, as well as Rousseau, of course, fixed on this drive as the basic flaw. It is rooted in our biological constitution (indeed Helvétius tried to reduce the psychological to the physical), but is quite distinct from it. A phenomenon of individualism, it exists, as Rousseau made explicit, only as the ungovernable child of the social order that is called into existence precisely to control or suppress the disorder of the biological or "natural" component of human nature. The fundamental paradox, if not the unresolvable dilemma is, then, that society, our very instrument for creating order, calls forth new and powerful forces of disorder. This is one of Rousseau's great developments, and we see it reflected, however wanly, in Diderot.

> In the so-called state of pure nature, men were scattered over the earth's surface like an infinite number of isolated little springs. From time to time it happened that some of these little springs encountered each other, pressed each other too strongly and broke. The legislators, witnessing these accidents, sought a remedy for them, and what is the remedy they imagined? To bring the little springs closer together, to compose out of them a beautiful machine which they called society. In the beautiful machine, society, the little springs, animated by an infinity of diverse and opposing interests, have acted and reacted against each other with all their strength, and, because of a moment of accidental warfare, they have established a true and continuous state of war in which all the little springs, weakened and worn out, have not stopped complaining, and in which more are broken in one year than would have been broken in ten in the primitive, isolated state in which the only law for a clash was personal resentment.[19]

How to deal with this problem, in a radical fashion, was beyond Diderot's abilities. He can approach it only on the level of weak abstractions. In the *Supplément au Voyage de Bougainville,* he gives us the rather trite and really quite meaningless notion that if laws did not violate nature they would be obeyed. Intended or not, this is a prescription for anarchy and a misunderstanding

[19] *Oeuvres politiques,* p. 303.

of the function of law, as well as a formula devoid of concrete substance, as we have already seen.

Diderot's article, "Droit naturel" (1755), to which we must again refer, was a purely theoretical attempt to establish the basis for obligation, and so to refute the claim of the refractory egoist—we may also call him nihilist or anarchist—that his natural desire for happiness, even at the expense of others, has priority over arbitrary and artificial social impositions. This argument recurs in France from the 1740's, on, in the subcurrent of immoralism, and Diderot, like other philosophers, was concerned with refuting it when he did not play with it in the seclusion of his study. Rousseau gave the problem a more lapidary formulation in *Emile,* where he says that each man regards himself as the center of the universe and orders all others in relation to himself—this being the very principle of disorder. In "Droit naturel," Diderot does not set up a straw man. He expounds the rebel's arguments in all their force, then draws on all the resources of his logic to counter them. His argument, we recall, posits a "general society of mankind." It possesses a general will prior to civil society, based on the identity of human nature. This notion is equivalent to a secular natural law. The rebel's self-justification implies both a law of reciprocity and a desire to be equitable; it rests in turn on the inevitability of man's being a reasoning animal, compelled by his nature to seek the truth and the right. If an individual refuses to, he renounces his human status, and society has the right to destroy him as it would a wild beast.

Diderot's argument lacks both logical and empirical certitude, and he never returned to this type of reasoning. It does not confound the resolute immoralist who chooses to live beyond good and evil, who refuses to overcome his present self. As Hume put it, there is no way of convincing a man, by rational argument, that he ought to be virtuous. We have noted that Rousseau's refutation was overwhelming. In addition to showing how unfounded Diderot's assumptions are, he adroitly contends that Diderot has placed himself on the wrong grounds for the accomplishment of his purpose. You cannot refute the argument of nature by appealing to nature (even assuming that Diderot's natural order exists). On that ground Diderot's nihilist is entirely right. Nature does not impel us to surrender our gratifications for the sake of others. It tells us to place ourselves first. There is no pragmatic value in appealing to the sense of justice. But there is an answer to the problem, if we recognize that the disorder is really social, not natural. The cause of social disorder and of alienation (inner disorder), for Rousseau, is an exploitative, competitive society, which gives every incentive for anarchic behavior. The answer lies not in rational argumentation nor on the moral plane. There can be only a political solution, one that totally remakes individual motivation, the character of society, and the relation between it and the individual.

Diderot's weakness as a political philosopher lies partly in his inability to cut through this basic antithesis of the human condition to a new ground on which it can be surpassed. His later writings, moreover, are often inconsistent with the suppositions of "Droit naturel." Not only do some of the fictional characters who carry out his intellectual explorations argue in contrary fashion, but his own theorizing both embodies and glides over the dilemma of the natural-social dualism. To cite one instance, in the *Entretiens avec Catherine II*, "There is only one duty, to be happy. Since my natural, invincible, inalienable inclination is to be happy, that is the source, and the only source of my true duties, and the only basis of good legislation."[20] More than once he declares that to be just is the only virtue, to be happy the only duty. The weakness of this kind of formula is in its refusal to contemplate the possible consequence, that "duty" and justice may become contraries.

Although another formulation of this idea, "I should desire, then, that the notion of happiness would be the fundamental basis of the civil catechism,"[21] may recall a famous phrase of the American Declaration of Independence, the preceding quotation points up the superficiality of the resemblance. Diderot's statement goes far beyond the idea that a government should promote individual happiness, an inalienable right. While its possible anarchistic implications are probably not intended (at this point, at least), the explicit intention also involves an implication far more radical than that of the Declaration of Independence: "And then, there are three distinct kinds of laws: nature's laws, the civil law, and the religious. The first should be the model of the other two, for otherwise they contradict each other, and good-bye morals." The illusion that a well-organized society merely continues and reaffirms that which is simply natural was one that Montesquieu, Rousseau, and other great political thinkers of the age rejected. Diderot's naïveté is all too evident:

[20] Ibid., pp. 320-21. See also p. 315, for a similar statement, and Jacques' "un homme heureux est sage" (*Oeuvres romanesques*, p. 503).

[21] *Oeuvres politiques*, p. 322. See also on p. 371, another formulation of the same idea.

> Nature has made all the good laws, the legislator announces them. I should urge on sovereigns: "If you want your laws to be observed, let them never contradict nature . . ." I want to be happy—this is the first article of a code prior to any legislation, to any religious system.[22]

When Diderot is writing as a moralist, or taking the role of his public *persona,* his consistent, repeated solution (like d'Holbach's) is the argument that only virtue brings happiness. "Of course the notion of duty must be sought in that of individual happiness. A wicked man is one who wants his happiness, and who does the opposite of what he wants. He sees no farther than his nose; he calculates badly."[23] That this attempted reconciliation of nature and culture is unsuccessful, that it embodies underlying anarchic elements, is obvious when Diderot writes: "This 'I' wants to be happy. This unchanging inclination is the eternal, permanent source of all its duties, even the most minute. Any contravening law is a crime of *lèse-humanité,* an act of tyranny."[24]

The idea that virtue and happiness are equivalents and the supposition that happiness, which can only be determined by each individual in his own way, can be the objective ground for personal morality and social order are quite appalling. They open the door to the immoralist or nihilist whom Diderot had tried to refute, and there is ample evidence that he realized this.

[22] Ibid., p. 371. For a contrary view, see A. M. Wilson, "The Development and Scope of Diderot's Political Thought," in *Studies on Voltaire and the Eighteenth Century,* vol. XXVII (1963), pp. 1887-88.

[23] *Commentaire sur la "Lettre sur l'homme et ses rapports,"* in *Oeuvres complètes,* ed. R. Lewinter, XI, 67.

[24] Ibid., p. 59.

> . . . any philosophy contrary to the nature of man is absurd, as is any legislation by which the citizen is continually forced to sacrifice his tastes and his happiness for the good of society. I, too, want society to be happy; but I want to be happy, too, and there are as many ways of being happy as there are individuals. Our own happiness is the basis of all our true duties.[25]

Diderot's words express the basic dilemma of eighteenth-century ethical thought, one which it could never resolve satisfactorily. A statement such as this must ultimately annul the constructive work of organizing an effective, functional society. It contradicts what he has said in favor of "a true notion of society," and the argumentation of "Droit naturel": "We want to be happy; but we are men and have no other rights that are truly inalienable except those of mankind" (XIV, 297). This conflict within Diderot, as we are about to see, will become even sharper in his wrestling with another question, whether a man can ever place himself above the law. Of less serious import in appearance only is his prescription for an ideal state, recalling Rabelais, or "Lui" in *Le Neveu de Rameau,* one in which there would be free reign for "all those charming vices that make man's happiness in this world and his eternal damnation in the next. . . . Let it all turn out as it will."[26]

The anarchic, disorderly element is present, then, in Diderot's politics, as well as his ethics. How seriously we should take the *Supplément au Voyage de Bougainville* has been debated by scholars. It suffices to recognize

[25] *Oeuvres politiques,* p. 404.
[26] Ibid., pp. 295-96; *idem,* p. 404.

that it continues a persistent thread. The native's argument against prohibition of incest is nothing but a denial of any structure, or an order of values.[27] Values have been established by nature. It cheerfully overlooks the need Diderot elsewhere recognizes to make moral and social distinctions that are not natural, but which it is natural for men to make. The sharp separation between "natural" and "artificial" is unreal.[28] It serves as a pretext for denying the transcendence of culture over nature, as we see in the deprecatory remark, "le reste est d'institution."[29]

This current of Diderot's thought is comparable to *the disintegrating forces of nature. It stands in opposi*tion to order, which at other moments he knows to be man's valuable and necessary conquest, on the grounds that order crushes the individual, who alone matters.

> I appeal to all institutions, civil and religious. Examine them profoundly: either I am entirely mistaken, or you will see mankind bent from century to century under a yoke that a handful of knaves conspired to impose on it. Distrust him who wants to put order into things. To make order is always to make oneself the master of others by constraining them. . . .[30]

[27] *Oeuvres philosophiques*, p. 496.

[28] L. G. Crocker, *Nature and Culture*, pp. 503-505.

[29] *Oeuvres philosophiques*, p. 507.

[30] Ibid., p. 512. In pushing his ideas to their extreme consequences, as was his wont, Diderot even goes so far as to contradict a basic element of his philosophy and to attribute to nature a moral purpose: "Its eternal will is that good should be preferred to evil, and the general good to the private" (p. 482). The argument of naturalistic providentialism (assuming Diderot believed it) is hardly an effective antidote.

Diderot occasionally lays emphasis on certain particulars that foment disorder. These are only manifestations, often local, of the basic aggressiveness. "Autorité politique" asserts that, in the establishment of society, violence or the *loi du plus fort* may usurp the authority that can be properly accorded only by agreement.[31] Diderot is aware of the ruthless economic exploitation of the poor, though it was still in its dawn, and it excites his wrath. The inhumanity of the life of mine-workers is a rather different thing from the hunger of the brutalized peasantry as described by La Bruyère.[32] But he sees no remedy, for to close the mines would bring ruin to the state and to many who depend on their products. Under the tutelage of Galiani he came to realize the abuse of economic power in the grain trade and the cruel disorder promoted by the complete laissez-faire of the Physiocrats, which he had previously embraced as a form of liberty and property rights. On this issue, however, his thinking remains ambiguous and unclarified, since he several times continues to support laissez-faire.[33] The particular institutional and class abuses of the Ancien Régime are of course the main focus of his demands for reform.

Despotism he hated more than anything else. His animosity toward Frederick the Great and his biting though unpublished reply to that monarch's *Examen de l'Essai sur les préjugés* are well known. It was Frederick he had in mind when in the *Principes de politique des souverains* (1774) he cried out against the atrociousness of condemning an individual out of the fear that he might trouble the public order.[34] "To deal harshly with

[31] *Oeuvres politiques,* pp. 9-10.

[32] Ibid., pp. 471-72.

[33] Ibid., pp. 403, 416.

[34] Ibid., p. 159.

the innocent when necessary: there is no honest man who cannot be intimidated by this maxim, which is unfailingly given the color of public interest."[35] With Catherine he compromised his intellectual honesty for the sake of personal interest (thus ironically testifying to his own critique of society), and perhaps in the illusion that he could persuade her to follow a better course.

Whereas Hobbes had seen despotic rule as the only possibility of overcoming human unruliness and the state of war of each against all, to Diderot it was clear that despotism was only a false order that propagated new forms of disorder. Tyranny—like anarchism—is a form of increasing entropy. When the value of the individual approaches zero, order becomes the illusory mask of disorder. In "Autorité politique" his criticism is abstract and limited. But already it is associated in his mind with the notion of inalienable rights: "to surrender one's heart, mind and conduct without any reservation to the will and caprice of a mere creature, to make him the only and final motive of one's actions, that is surely a crime of divine *lèse-majesté*. . . . True and legitimate power, therefore, is necessarily limited."[36] Rousseau, also opposed to despots, will demand precisely such an absolute submission to the general will. But Diderot's concept of the contract, which is the limit in right to authority, is a feeble barrier. For him the sovereign *is* the ruler, in actuality if not in the origination of things; the contract, which has alienated sovereignty to him, requires only that he not transfer it to someone else. Sovereignty returns to the people only when the royal line is extinct. By its nature it binds the subjects to absolute obedience, after all. They are obliged "to honor and fear their master as the one through whom they

[35] Ibid., p. 163.

[36] Ibid., p. 12.

have wanted the image of God to be present and visible to them on earth."[37] Resistance and revolution are never justified, no matter how unjust their king.

It is easy to claim that Diderot's words in the *Encyclopédie* are precautionary, perhaps even an Aesopian language designed to convey the opposite of what they say. We do not know, even as we are not sure how much of the article is his, how much was cribbed. It remains that it offers nothing positive as a limit or a remedy and that his concept of the contract is consonant with this weakness.

In the 1770's, when Diderot moves to harder and more radical positions, he speaks in a different voice. To be sure, he speaks only to himself, to Catherine's private ear, and to posterity. To the public of his own time, unlike the heroic or foolhardy Citizen of Geneva, he was mute. In his private writings, he denounces monarchs as the true atheists who trample on all laws, divine and human, in their need to be feared by their subjects.[38] Nothing excited him more than the dismissal and exile of the Parlements in January 1771. For him and for many other *philosophes* this was the crisis of the monarchy, its passage from the last vestige of limit to sheer absolutism. You have seen, he exclaims to Catherine, "the rape and the destruction of the depository of our fundamental laws."[39] Some, like Voltaire, saw the Parlements for the largely futile and almost wholly selfish vested interest-group that they were. Diderot was not at all blind to their defects. The Parlement's prerogative of registering laws "has only a frivolous origin, has produced almost no good. . . ."[40] It is a tribunal, he tells Catherine, "in which Your Majesty will certainly

[37] Ibid., p. 20. [38] Ibid., p. 194. [39] Ibid., p. 362.
[40] Ibid., p. 234.

not recognize any of the characteristics of a barrier projected for the defense of peoples against the arbitrary power of an imbecile or wicked sovereign."[41] It is wrong, then, to claim that Diderot erred in his judgment of this institution. But it was an institution, the only one of its kind. To Diderot what seemed important was that the forms of legality were destroyed, the last remnant of the unwritten constitution swept away.

Even in the *Entretiens avec Catherine II*, which are relatively prudent, Diderot points a lesson to her when he discusses French history. The first mistake was when the French entrusted the entire public power to the king, in order to assure execution of the laws. "That is the first fault, the original sin."[42] Such authority, he declares, is inevitably extended beyond its original intent. Kings soon forget that it is only "a deposit." Their arrogation of power assumes the right to change or to make laws, which belonged to councils or assemblies. Vernière has appropriately called this version of French history "ces rêveries." Diderot's vocabulary, moreover, reveals that he has made no progress in his concept of sovereignty. The first kings, he writes, "realized that it did not belong to sovereign authority to meddle with legislation"—that is, it was not something belonging to the king, in whom sovereignty inheres. Diderot, then, upholds two coexistent claims: "sovereign authority" and "the inalienable privileges of a nation."[43] Nevertheless, in the *Observations sur le Nakaz* and the *Réfutation d'Helvétius*, he is firmer in his insistence on freedom and inalienable rights, which can be protected only by constant vigilance, by "that continual vigilance ('*alarme*'), the indispensable preserver of liberty."[44]

[41] Ibid., p. 245. [42] Ibid., p. 222. [43] Ibid., p. 224.
[44] Ibid., pp. 354-55.

How can we reconcile two claims, each of which is or tends to be absolute? Will not their clash be productive of the disorder that government exists to obviate? Diderot apparently believes that the clash and the disorder stem from the second great error in French history. This was the failure of Charles VII to sweep away the confusion of customary law (which Diderot, in the Cartesian spirit, detests) and to institute "a uniform and general code. He did not do it, and that failure is beyond remedying. France is condemned never to have a code."[45] Why never? Because destruction of the "monstrous colossus" of customary law would shake established property rights and cause widespread injustices. And Diderot did not really want to do that. Such a change, he believed, was beyond mere reform. It meant a revolution. About that he was right.

There are, to be sure, occasional moments when he speaks of a revolution as possible or inevitable. In *Observations sur le Nakaz*: "The bounds of suffering or oppression are set by nature"; when people are dying of hunger, "that is the time of revolt."[46] And in the *Réfutation d'Helvétius*: "I was asked one day how you can restore morals among a corrupt people. I replied: 'In the same way Medea restored her father's youth, by cutting him up and boiling him.' "[47] This is mere rhetoric, an abstract notion whose reality would have frightened him. Diderot, like Rousseau, was no friend of revolution. Like other successful *philosophes*, he had become part of the Establishment and profited from its favors as well as from the financial possibilities of nascent industrialism. If he wished to reform the regime extensively, indeed radically, it was from within the

[45] Ibid., p. 224. [46] Ibid., p. 380.

[47] *Oeuvres philosophiques*, p. 466.

Establishment, and as a way of insuring its survival through adaptive change.

The best way, then, to assure both the rights of authority and the rights of liberty is to establish a constitution, a "code," with impregnable safeguards:

> In any country whatsoever, the authority of the sovereign must therefore be limited, and limited in a lasting way. The difficult problem to solve is not, then, to give a people laws or even good laws, but to protect these laws from any attack on the part of the sovereign....
>
> Since according to the natural order there are twenty fools for one wise man, a good government is one in which the liberty of individuals is restricted as little as possible, and that of the sovereign as much as possible.[48]
>
> If there is any disadvantage to be feared, it is not that the monarch will forget his prerogative, but that the subjects will forget their rights.[49]

For this reason, benevolent despotism is deadly. A succession of benevolent despots would make the people forget "their inalienable rights; they would fall into a fatal security and apathy."[50] Diderot twice repeated this favorite idea.

The secret of social order, then, lies in a government of laws. Rousseau had expressed the same idea, and in a moment of pessimism declared its realization to be a problem as impossible of solution as the quadrature of the circle. He at least made the effort, and wrote the *Contrat social.* Beyond the demand for reform of abuses, Diderot gives us only a general idea of what a good

[48] *Oeuvres politiques,* p. 355.

[49] Ibid., p. 362.

[50] Ibid., p. 355.

constitution and good political institutions would be like. Neither philosopher attempts to indicate a way of setting them up in the present situation. The best Diderot can do is this piece of advice to Catherine, concerning her own projects for Russia:

> It would be suitable to specify the rights of the *intermediary powers* and to fix them irrevocably for the legislator himself and for his successors. If they are dependent on the supreme power, they are nothing. A free people differs from a people of slaves only by the inalienability of certain privileges belonging to man as man; to each class of citizens as a member of that class, and to each citizen as a member of society. There are neither rights, nor laws, nor liberty where the sovereign can do as he wills with rights and laws. . . . I know only three or four ways: knowledge or public education, brevity of the code and the laws, education, an oath of national loyalty, and the periodical assembly of the Estates-General; but above all, education and the enjoyment [of rights or laws] confirmed by a long passage of time.[51]

Diderot never indicated a belief that such a program was possible for his own country, and he avoided expressing himself publicly on any of these matters.

In law he saw the principal hope for an orderly society. It must be obeyed, whether or not it is a good law. Here he seems close to Montaigne and Pascal for whom the law was sacrosanct in its own majesty; but he never says, like Rousseau, that whatever the law commands is just. It may be criticized, but it must be obeyed.

In the privacy of his study, in his "doctrine secrète,"

[51] Ibid., p. 360.

he played with the idea that the exceptional man may take it into his own hands to put justice above the law. He had already raised this question in the *Salon de 1767*. Is virtue, he asks, "the habit of conforming one's conduct to the law, or rather, the habit of conforming one's conduct to public utility?"[52] The answer, Diderot replies without hesitation, is the first. The second is "the virtue of the legislator or the sovereign . . . for who has a precise idea of public utility?"

How can we justify asking a sensible man to override his conscience? Bad usages, Diderot argues, cannot last. We must, if need be, choose to be a good citizen rather than a good man—the fault will be the law's, and we must protest against it, try to change it. He sees the complexities of the problem, which is perennial and still a lively issue. What if the law itself prohibits such protest, even makes it a capital crime? "I shall remain silent or move away." But he must obey the law, "for fear that by disputing, on my own private authority, bad laws, I may by my example encourage the insensate to dispute good ones."

Diderot comes down hard on the side of order, but the question, as he admits, tormented him and so he returned to it in the *Entretien d'un père avec ses enfants* (1771) and in the *Entretiens avec Catherine II*. In the former, the father supports unswerving obedience as necessary to order, while the son pleads exception for the exceptional man. In the second work, Diderot defines the exceptional man as the *philosophe,* who alone, like the legislator or the king, really can rise above personal interest and recognize the general interest.[53] Still, as Diderot the citizen, he cannot really

[52] *Oeuvres complètes,* XI, 121-23.

[53] *Oeuvres politiques,* p. 321.

approve, and in the *Supplément au Voyage de Bougainville* (1772) he again refuses to allow exceptions.[54]

In other words, the determination of the general interest, that is, the formulation of law, must be entrusted to the king or to a legislative body. We may note in passing that in the *Principes de politique des souverains* (1774) Diderot turns this into an accusation against despots: "Always to respect the law that does not hinder us and which hinders others. It would be better to respect them all."[55] Here is another problem. But if the king cannot be trusted, neither can the people. If we were to ask individuals to determine their actions according to their own notions of the general interest, then "ignorance and self-interest, which becloud everything in human heads, will show the general interest to be where it is not. Each having his own virtue, men's lives will be filled with crimes."[56] Although Diderot's conception of society, government, and liberty are antithetical to those of Rousseau, we see that once again they are in agreement on these starting points. Diderot puts the argument for law even more vividly in the *Entretiens avec Catherine II*:

> Abolish the civil law in a capital for just one year. The indigent will hurl themselves upon the rich. The latter will take up arms to defend their property. Blood will flow in the streets. The city will present the frightening image of what will go on and must go on in the whole world. . . . There will be wars, truces, peace treaties; everything will be done out of fear and ambition and self-interest. It is a lamentable but inevitable condition, among beings who have no

[54] Ibid., p. 321 n.
[55] Ibid., p. 168.
[56] *Oeuvres complètes*, XI, 121.

tribunal where they can be judged. They are, like the tiger and the wolf, in the state of nature.[57]

His thinking proceeds further. Though order requires obedience to law, good or bad, from his remarks on the *Nakaz* it would seem that he comes to the view that obedience is only a necessary, but not the sufficient condition for order. Like almost all the philosophes (Rousseau being the notable exception), he thought that a people's mores are determined (and therefore may be changed) by its laws. "I think that morals are the consequence of laws."[58] "There are no morals, constant and general, but those having legislation as their basis."[59] This being so, bad laws will produce bad mores, and so the rule of law will not be adequate to the purpose. "Morals are good when the laws which are observed are good, bad when they are bad. When the laws, good or bad, are not observed, there are no morals."[60] Diderot embraces another naïve cliché of his time: all that is necessary is to arrange things so that evil actions are self-punishing, "which will always happen if the welfare and the ills of society are indivisibly linked with the welfare and the ills of those who compose it."[61] In Rousseau's mind, this simplistic truism was to assume a different, complex—to some, a terrifying—shape.

The only way to assure the rule of law—Diderot returns to this point—is to have a written code or constitution. Without it, a nation will follow "the chance impulsion of circumstances which give rise to crazy, absurd, contradictory institutions; institutions that in time develop such extensive roots that it becomes im-

[57] *Oeuvres politiques*, p. 317.

[58] Ibid., p. 372. [59] Ibid., p. 376. [60] Ibid., p. 372.

[61] Ibid., p. 376.

possible to cut them off."[62] Usage, after centuries go by, is tantamount to confusion. Chance and planlessness are antithetical to order.[63] A code has certainty. It can and should be placed in the hands of every child and used as a catechism.[64] It can help to safeguard the most precious concession a ruler can make—the gift of part of his authority, the barrier against despotism (228).[65] The concession Diderot urges Catherine to make takes the form of a permanent legislative body with severely limited powers.[66] Such a body would enable the general interest to prevail. Diderot seems to grasp the democratic process in a liberal society, but his phrase is not really clear: "In the concourse and conflict of general wills and private wills lies the special advantage of democracy over all other kinds of government"—disorder working its way to order through orderly process.[67]

The course of history shows that nations inevitably decline, order falls into disorder. In a previously quoted passage, Diderot says, "The word 'society' suggests a state of union."[68] This is the work of structuring, of building an imitation of a complex natural organism. Because the attempt is human, because it is flawed by the human dichotomies and imperfections, "the thing is exactly the contrary, it is a state of war." The structure, like all others, contains its built-in forces of disintegration. And

[62] Ibid., p. 256. [63] Ibid., p. 231. [64] Ibid., p. 223.

[65] In the *Entretiens*, Diderot is still being cautious. In the *Nakaz* we see that he considered the "gift" to be something that belongs to a people. Even in the *Entretiens* he insists that the body of the people must take an active part in the pact if it is to work (p. 248). In the *Nakaz*, he has the monarch taking an oath appended to each law, and urges a representative assembly to judge the monarch every five years, to continue him in office or depose him (pp. 343-44).

[66] Ibid., pp. 274-77. [67] Ibid., p. 276. [68] Ibid., p. 401.

so he goes on to say, making the analogy quite specific, "In morals as in physics, it is easier to go down than to go up again." Increasing entropy, or degradation of ordered energy, eventually wins.

Only wise laws and institutions can retard this natural law.[69] But they can do no more than that. In the article "Hobbisme," Diderot looks for a middle path between the systems of Hobbes and Rousseau: "although the condition of mankind is one of perpetual mutability, its goodness and wickedness are the same, its happiness and unhappiness circumscribed by limits it cannot exceed. All artificial advantages are paid for, all natural ills compensated."[70] War is as inevitable as faithless, immoral, and inhumane rulers: "study of the human heart and the experience of all the centuries prove to me that they are what they should be, because it takes only one wicked man to force the hand of all the good."[71]

It is no different with Diderot's hope that laws can arrange a coincidence between the general and private interests, so that the wicked man cannot harm society without hurting himself. Returning to the realism of Rousseau, and of Rameau's nephew, he writes despondently in *Observations sur le Nakaz*: "The wicked man knows that: but what he knows even better is that he gains more by being wicked than he loses as a member of the society he is harming." There is no solution. "There is and there will always be circumstances from which an evildoer can profit, and in which there is no relation between the benefit he gets as an evildoer and the hurt he does himself as a citizen."[72]

Now he even goes back on his faith in a fixed written

[69] Ibid., p. 242.

[70] *Oeuvres complètes,* XV, 122-23.

[71] *Oeuvres politiques,* p. 319. [72] Ibid., p. 352.

code: "Positive laws are just as eternal and universal"—since they are corollaries of natural laws. "Nevertheless it is certain that a given positive law is good and useful in one circumstance, harmful and bad in another; it is certain that there is no code that does not have to be reformed with the passage of time. This difficulty may not be insolvable; but it must be solved."[73] But it may be insolvable—in fact the whole political problem may be insolvable. Whatever precautions we may take to assure the rule of law and equality before the law, they will fail. "That should be so, that has always been assumed, but that has never been, and perhaps it has never been possible for it to be so."[74] The value of enlightenment is after all limited: "Nevertheless, we must enlighten and instruct, but not expect too much from this means."[75] He even doubts the validity of his own role:

> We could be consoled for ills past and present, if the future held the promise of changing this destiny. But it is impossible to lull ourselves with such a hope; and if you asked the philosopher of what use are the counsels he persists in addressing to the nations and their rulers, and if he replied with sincerity, he would say that he is satisfying an invincible inclination to speak the truth, at the risk of arousing indignation and even of drinking in Socrates' cup.[76]

[73] Ibid., p. 353. [74] Ibid., p. 366. [75] Ibid., p. 359.

[76] Ibid., p. 367. Cf. an analogous passage later on, in which, speaking of the long cry of the oppressed and the demonstration by modern philosophers of the tacit social pact, of inalienable rights to freedom and property, he asks: "What have they accomplished? Nothing. Amidst the demands of all civilized peoples, voiced by magistrates and philosophers, despotism spreads its sway on all sides" (p. 405).

The difficulties are augmented when bad institutions are old and deeply rooted. Like Rousseau, he exclaims, "How lucky is a people that is starting out fresh."[77] And he is led once more to speculate that, after all, a revolution may be necessary. If so, then the *philosophe* has a definite role to play in the process, which he describes in tones reminiscent of Etienne de La Boëtie:

> He tells the people that they are the stronger and that, if they go to the slaughter, it is because they let themselves be led to it. He prepares for revolutions, which always occur when misery becomes extreme, an aftermath that compensates for the bloodshed.[78]

Revolution, the supreme disorder, is a culmination of intolerable disorder. Wisely prepared and guided, it may lead to a better order. As I have suggested, one cannot say that Diderot, the successful *philosophe* who enjoyed many of the benefits of the Establishment, looked forward to such a cataclysm. The prospect of revolution could be intellectually enticing, especially at the thought of injustice and exploitation, but, deep down, he would not have wanted it in his time.[79]

Particularly striking is the embodiment in Diderot's own personality of the same antithesis of order and disorder. It is evident in his life. In his moral and political speculations, anarchic tendencies frequently raise their head against his love of order. The latter is without question the more serious, the more fundamental belief.

> Do you want me to tell you a pretty paradox? I am convinced that there can be no real happiness for mankind except in a social state in which there would

[77] Ibid., p. 225. [78] Ibid., p. 320.

[79] See R. Mortier, "Diderot anti-colonialiste," *Revue belge de philologie et d'histoire*, vol. XLIX (1971), pp. 897, 901.

> be no king, nor magistrate, nor priest, nor laws, nor thine, nor mine, nor personal property, nor real property, nor vices, nor virtues. And that social state is devilishly ideal.[80]

Diderot's occasional primitivism takes the shape of anarchic individualism. Viewed in another perspective, it is a form of conservatism, or reaction, in its longing for a return to the past, to a static state of perfection. This is again profoundly contradictory, though in a different way, to his general theory of social construction and order. Such primitivism is a dream of avoiding the tension and conflict that are not only the conditions of progress (which at such moments he longs to halt) but also the embodiment, within the human condition, of the constructive and destructive antithesis through which change, the law of all being, operates. Change is a law of history, because cause and effect do not cease to operate in the human realm as in all else. The course of history, like the sun, cannot be arrested.

> He has perhaps pushed his victory much further than was good for his happiness; for between the arrowhead and the Chinese porcelain there is a long run. But everything is linked in a chain, starting with the first spurt of the human mind. It is impossible to guess where it will stop.[81]

The weakness of Diderot's political thought, according to Robert Niklaus, lies "in his failure to relate the self-centered, anarchical man to the moral and political structure of society."[82] To put the same idea differently,

[80] *Le Temple du bonheur*, in *Oeuvres complètes*, VI, 439.

[81] *Oeuvres politiques*, pp. 304-305.

[82] R. Niklaus, *A Literary History of France. The Eighteenth Century. 1715-1789*, London and New York, 1970, p. 232.

he never solves the essential question that Rousseau addressed so decisively: Is there a general interest separate from the sum of individual interests? The reply is affirmative if we postulate, like Rousseau, an organic whole emerging from the conglomeration of units. In that case—to use Diderot's own mode of thinking, which he did not apply thoroughly and consistently in the social sphere—the individuals, like the organs of the body, have their own self-interest, but must submit to the harmony of the whole organism. The organism has a distinct reality, a self-interest and a will of its own. Unless they prevail, anarchy and disintegration ensue. Diderot goes part of the way when, after realizing that moral limits cannot be rationally justified, he makes of morals "une affaire de police," and affirms that the general interest is the rule of right and wrong.[88] But equally dear to him are the freedom and dignity of the individual. He knows, despite his moralism, that happiness depends in a large measure on the satisfaction of instinctual demands that are anarchic, and so productive of disorder. His insistence on individual rights signifies both his willingness to allow a certain amount of disorder and his awareness of the cost of ideal, utopian societies in which order is theoretically perfect.

We cannot censure Diderot for leaving the matter unresolved. Such a state, fluctuating and open, is the very condition of a free society. It represents also a consistent application to human affairs of the idea of a continuing, universal struggle between order and disorder. His stature as a political thinker is nonetheless damaged by his failure to face this issue in a consistent, direct way and to formulate some kind of overall theory,

[88] See J. Proust, *Diderot et l'Encyclopédie,* Paris, 1962, pp. 320, 401-402.

some more precise answer to the fundamental political question, the relation of the sentient, egocentric individual to the political and moral structures of culture.

In sum, Diderot's ideas and attitudes veered, after 1770, toward a more radical critical stance, and toward a liberal society based on a fixed constitution and code of laws, and the inalienable rights of citizens. Despite some concrete proposals for reform, he never developed a full and consistent theory of the good state. If, like Rousseau, he saw society as a state of war, he did not envision any way of ending it, and hoped only that it could be attenuated. His hesitations and alternations are striking. The problems of order and freedom are constant preoccupations, but he is in turn naïve, vague, and pessimistic in regard to their solution. He does know their enemies: stupidity, selfishness, the lust for power, and the eternal vicissitudes of life. As in nature, the struggle for order is unending. The children of light can never eliminate the children of darkness. But Diderot could not for a moment give up the struggle to move closer to freedom, justice, and order, and to resist—within the bounds of prudence—their antagonists. It is his inability to find a solution convincing to himself or available in a real situation that leads to his discouragement. And if our view of Diderot's wrestling with the problems of order and disorder in the domain of political philosophy seems to have shown it to be less satisfying or exciting than his thinking in the other three spheres, the reason for it is the relative insubstantiality, incoherence, and unoriginality that limit his accomplishment.

Conclusion

"After a little, it first struck me that I yet comprehended nothing; and here I was right; for the connection of the parts with each other was entirely unknown to me, and everything depends on that."

Wilhelm Meister's Apprenticeship

A REREADING OF THE FOREGOING CHAPters leaves this writer with one outstanding impression. In studying the role of order and disorder as persistent and guiding directives of Diderot's thought, it has not been possible to separate metaphysics, natural philosophy, morals, politics, and aesthetics into self-contained subjects. Each chapter has forced its indissoluble interconnections upon us. In other words, the theme of order and disorder has enabled us, whatever the faults of our treatment, to reach a truly synthetic view of Diderot's philosophy. The theme is not only omnipresent, it correlates and unifies an attitude and an outlook, a way of apprehending reality, life, and the many problems they present to man, who is bound to the perplexities of the human condition.

Diderot's attempt to fathom the ultimate reality of the cosmos led him to a view of universal process and law. The categories of the human mind obliged him to inquire whether the world is a rational harmony, a rational structure, a logical necessity, a coherent system.

Rational causes are those that are understandable to the human reason, in terms of the structures of thought and its modes of operation. He knew that these are limited and do not correspond to the fullness of reality. Thus determinism was necessary to his world-system; but human life reveals another dimension of existence, evolves on its own level of law.

In other ways, too, what he found was both enigmatic and disturbing to the reason. In one sense the universal law of cause and effect, of structuring and disintegration, is coherent and logically understandable. In another sense, the process itself, even when an order results, is disorderly, unstable, without plan, purpose or meaning, profoundly irrational to the human understanding. Important consequences follow. Religion and the deity are eliminated. The scientific enterprise is seen to fabricate an order of its own, not false but incomplete and ephemeral, by the abstraction of phenomena amenable to its methods. But nature itself, if we go beyond, far from being a perfect machine or a rational system, remains a savage, mysterious chaos.

Some natural phenomena are manifestly rational, especially mechanics. This explains the hold of mechanics on Diderot, and his tendency to explain biological phenomena, as far as possible, in terms of such mechanical causes as heat and movement. But many essential phenomena, especially organism and life itself, could not be so explained. He knew that the conceptions he elaborates went beyond rational or empirical justification, and he offers them only as conjectures. But he assumes there are justifications unknown to us. An explanation of phenomena in rational terms, such as celestial mechanics, substantiates a universe of orderly process. On the other hand, the introduction of time and becoming, of process and change, injects disorderly elements—the evolution of worlds, the production of animals and monsters, leading to the central conclusion of an order of disorder.

We have in the twentieth century come closer to an understanding of phenomenal realities, but only by surpassing the limits of rational conceptualizations, by a new awareness that reality cannot be comprehended in conventionally rational images. Relativity allows and embraces rational contradiction. It posits a universe both finite and unbounded, having a beginning without having begun, filled with energy without the need of a creator to account for it. On the microscopic scale, it is no longer thought possible to know whether what is observed is in matter or in the structures of our thought.[1]

Diderot intuited some of these limits. He knew that to reduce reality to the rational is to reduce it to the human. It follows that the questions of order and disorder, so intrinsic to human rationality, cannot be answered in completely objective terms, since their very essence and definition is what the mind conceives of as rational and irrational.

Still, the conception of process Diderot gradually achieves does provide a workable, if incomplete, understanding of natural events, and especially of the most baffling of these, life itself. It delineates the basic problems of the moral life, by establishing "a metaphysical flux which would imply a correlative ethical flux."[2] The metaphysical ground of moral values had long rested on the divinely ordered Christian cosmos. Now it was sheared off. The essential problem is thus posed:

[1] J. Charron, *Cosmology*, London, 1970, pp. 13-15.

[2] S. Kabelac, *op. cit.*, p. 99.

Can we establish valid, efficacious ethics without a metaphysical ground, on a natural and social foundation?

Once put on this basis, the moral problem retains its negative relation with the metaphysical, but becomes inextricably involved with the political. The social "order" is false and productive of moral disorder. Two instances that concern Diderot particularly are the conventual system and marriage, but he sees social institutions in general, insofar as they stimulate the natural human drives for power and importance at the expense of others—the fount of aggressiveness—as engendering moral disorder. The temptation of anarchism is that of the dissolution of false orders and the liberation of the instinctual. Its contrary begins with the admission that evil is a necessary part of the world system, a subjective evaluation or one made by society, but indifferent in itself. From this viewpoint the validity of the distinction between right and wrong becomes trivial. However, a society, like any other structure, responds to the universal effort to resist disintegration. If anything may be called "right," or "a right," these words are attributable to the social structure at least as much as to individuals. The struggle against the evildoers becomes "une affaire de police," a social tyranny, an enforcement of decent human relations, of morality (which from this viewpoint is not denied), on grounds that are not themselves moral, but purely natural—precisely the grounds of the immoralist's refusal to subject himself to them.[3]

[3] It is also Diderot's hope that, following the causal law, punishment will be a deterrent, that it will "modify" the unsocial individual. The argument is specious, since the necessarily determined individual cannot help not being modified, or adequately

Morals are thus absorbed into politics. Although Diderot does not conceive the reply to the immoralist in the strictly and profoundly political terms of Rousseau's refutation of "Droit naturel," he emphasizes the dependency of morals on law and government. But morals are also indissociable from the aesthetic experiences. Not only because of the "holy trinity," "le bon, le vrai et le beau," but because Diderot is less interested in theory than in the concrete case or individual, which allows him to carry on his imaginary "moral experiments" as he observes, fascinated by his own creations, the spectacle of the play of forces.

The weakness of Diderot as moralist is his inability to extricate himself from the bog of the nature-culture antithesis and to find footing on firmer ground. Even within the narrow circle of the natural, the relative status of the individual and the species remains unclarified, the latter implying similarity or order, the former a claim against uniformities.

> Every being tends toward its happiness; and the happiness of one being cannot be the happiness of another. Morals, then, are enclosed within the circumference of the species. What is a species? A multitude of individuals organized in the same way. What! Organization the basis of morals! I do believe so.[4]

When we consider virtue as the synonym of order, and vice or evil as that of disorder, we are, Diderot knows, taking the anthropocentric point of view that confers value on acts according to their effects on others,

---

modified. Diderot is obliged to fall back on the phrases, "heureusement né," "malheureusement né."

[4] *Salon de 1767, Oeuvres complètes*, XI, 124.

and on social life in general. Men are both the object or victims of evil and the agents or causes of it. It is quite clear that for Diderot virtue is by definition a surpassing of the disorder created by the egoistic vitalities, for by themselves they can produce only disorder. Despite the fatal confusion of morals and happiness in Diderot's thinking—which at times leads him to the equation, "what is just is what makes me happy"—he praises altruism and self-sacrifice and attempts to justify them as the true path to happiness. At other times, he denies the very same claim as theoretical and empirical fallacies or illusions.

A further complication arises. His insistence on individual uniqueness in regard to happiness corresponds to his general idea of the emergence of individuality at the human level of cosmic evolution. At the same time, the primacy of the social implied by the idea of virtue is also justified by the universal ordering process and the tendency to seek stability in a viable structure. The inertia of stability is contrary to the dynamic law of things and to human nature itself, even as it coexists with it: "Together with a more or less considerable fund of inertia, Nature, who watches over our preservation, has given us a portion of energy that prods us constantly to movement and action."[5] These are conditions of existence, and they enfold man. On the other hand, man has no choice but to live in his own realm of moral judgment and valuation: "What is a man? An animal? Without doubt. But a dog is an animal, too; the wolf is an animal, too; but man is neither a wolf nor a dog."[6]

Thus Diderot takes two contrary viewpoints at different times, and they faithfully reflect the human dilemma. Seen one way, morality is a necessary, justifiable,

[5] Ibid., p. 219.

[6] Ibid., p. 124.

human order, a structure imposed on the disorderly energy of natural impulse. Seen another way, it is a disordering of the natural order. The respect of certain engagements, such as conjugal fidelity, substitutes for the natural order (such as it is) the disorder of repressed temptations, suffering, jealousy, unhappiness. Only a prior commitment to a moral order can make virtue a higher value than the satisfactions it denies. Even then, no moral code can go too far in contravening nature, or it will be ineffective and compound natural disorder with its own consequences, frustrating its very purposes.

Unlike Rousseau, Diderot conceives of no clear or rigorous solution to the dilemmas he propounds. He enounces no system of ethics. Man is compelled to live in a tenuous equilibrium, one that is really a state of flux, between two legitimate demands. Both the moralist and the politician must use their reason, skills, and practical insights to work out the best possible arrangements, theoretical and practical, for society and for the individuals who compose it, who are in the ambiguous position of being both its beneficiaries and its antagonists.[7]

Just as Diderot's cosmic speculations have as their starting point the question, Is the world a rational harmony?, so his political speculations center on the unspoken question, Can society be a rational harmony? Just as the ethical inquiry involves all other manifestations of the universal processes of order and disorder, so the search for polity cannot be separated from ethics and even, at an ultimate reach, from metaphysics. Politics is another approach to the same disorder or lack of

[7] For the insolubility of the problem of happiness in Diderot, see R. Mauzi, "Diderot et le bonheur," in *Diderot Studies III*, especially pp. 266-70.

harmony inherent in the conflict between nature and culture, between the rights of the individual, fully emerged in his own determined structure, and those of the "higher" structure that requires his subordination. In his political writings, Diderot is constantly asking questions such as these: What are the causes of disorder in our societies? Can order be brought about? What institutions would be most favorable to it, and especially to a just order?

In the political inquiry, the ethical conclusions, especially the view of man's nature and potentialities, are determining in shaping the kind of response, and ultimately, the institutions to effectuate it. The moral and the political problems both involve the mutual rights and duties of a multiplicity of "others" and their relation to the larger whole. In both spheres the efforts to construct and maintain an order are countered by the same disruptive forces of self-assertion. Virtue is rational behavior, defined as that which is favorable to the best possible order of general happiness; paradoxically, individual happiness may consist of disorderly (irrational) behavior. In the governance of men, the order of violence is denounced as a false and irrational order. The order of law (the rational order), however, is never attained, and society depends on violence to maintain itself.

The struggle to control political power and the acts of aggression and exploitation form the substance of a labyrinthine riddle that Diderot finds as baffling as the moral riddle. The best form of government allies the greatest stability with the greatest latitude of individual self-expression. Although Diderot sees the individual as a disruptive force, he does not, like Rousseau, consider political or civil liberty in itself to be a disorder in the social body. He does not accept Rousseau's definition, with its totalitarian implications, of a society as a true organism, like the human body. A society, like the universe itself, is a system of interacting forces, not an organic whole dependent for its survival on a harmony and a unity into which the parts are completely subsumed. As a humanist, Diderot is willing to sacrifice the dream of complete order and stability to the higher value of individual self-realization. For Rousseau, on the other hand, happiness and justice are contingent on the complete and unreserved socialization of the individual components.

It may be said that in both his moral and political philosophy, and especially in the political, Diderot flounders and vacillates. Nonetheless, he has the merit, many would claim, of seeing all sides, of not diminishing real complexities, of not embracing easy and rigid panaceas.

Diderot's shape of mind was hostile to the fanaticism and optimism of utopianism, and rejected its essentially static conceptualizations. Although he had no philosophy of history—Vernière affirms that he was "hostile à l'histoire"[8]—he does have an attitude toward history, considering it as one manifestation of his general concept of change as the law of being, of energy operating through combination, disintegration and reconstruction, in endless cycles. The state of the human species, he notes in the *Encyclopédie*, in the article "Hobbisme," is one of "vicissitude perpétuelle."[9] In 1778 he made this plea to the American insurgents: "May they postpone, at least for several centuries, the decree issued against all the things of this world; a decree that has

[8] *Oeuvres politiques*, p. XVI.

[9] *Oeuvres complètes*, XV, 122.

condemned them to have their birth, their period of flourishing, their decline and their end!"[10] Moreover, the events of history are like all others in their obedience to the law of causality. "A further secret contradiction is detected," remarks Roland Mortier; "the belief in a kind of internal necessity in history, formulated in almost fatalistic terms."[11] The contradiction, however, is not one peculiar to history. It joins history to the universal laws of all being, as Diderot has conceived them in his cosmic, biological, moral, and political philosophy. All process is chaotic, at least to the human eye and understanding, but, in an objective sense, necessary. The life of nations follows the same course of disorder-order-disorder that constitutes the universal "order" of things. It may well be that Diderot's avoidance of the problem of history and a philosophy of history reflects his awareness that history is not understandable in terms of a rational science. It is more perplexing even than the natural processes, which continue to operate in history, but are perturbed by a multiplicity of factors peculiar to the human level of motivation and conscious will.

Aesthetics, finally, is inextricably intertwined, in Diderot's thinking, with cosmic realities and with ethics. With the former, because the aesthetic harmony created by art must deal with disorder; with the latter, because that disorder is to a considerable extent moral, and because art's highest function is to help us understand disorder in human affairs and the value of moral order. In fiction and the theater, no art is possible that is not involved with these problems of life. The same tensions we have discussed are art's substance. "Between the ideal

[10] *Oeuvres politiques*, p. 491.

[11] R. Mortier, *op. cit.*, p. 900.

zone of virtue and that of sensual pleasures," writes Mauzi, "lies the immense field of the imaginary."[12] Or, as M. T. Cartwright puts it, the artist "imposes and justifies himself by aiming, through the expressive character of his work, at a definition of man and of his place in the world."[13]

Diderot's fiction is deeply concerned with the problem of finding new and better aesthetic processes to express the experience of human and cosmic disorder. He breaks out of the classical aesthetic imitation, which is "an expertly modeled representation of what *might* be a natural order," into forms that themselves have some kinship with anarchy, and that befit "an attitude toward the world which finds in experience no underlying reason but only a series of circumstances."[14] Although Diderot's theory usually expresses the classical aesthetics of "la belle nature," his own practice is quite different, and relies instead on fragmentation and dissonance. "To understand the genesis of Diderot's most living works," writes Yves Benot cleverly, "it is essential to estimate to what extent he wrote them *against* the dominant taste of his period, and against his own."[15]

We have emphasized *Jacques le Fataliste* as a remarkable and innovative aesthetic expression of metaphysical and human order and disorder, as Diderot conceived them. It is as if he were saying that form itself structures meaning; that the function of aesthetic creation is to organize its constructs so that they convey meaning;

[12] R. Mauzi, *op. cit.*, p. 284.

[13] M. T. Cartwright, *Diderot critique d'art et le problème de l'expression, Diderot Studies XIII*, Genève, 1969, p. 50.

[14] S. Kabelac, *op. cit.*, pp. 104-105.

[15] Yves Benot, *Diderot, de l'athéisme à l'anticolonialisme*, Paris, 1970, p. 90.

and that, since experience itself is disorganized, art must reflect that reality if it is to be a true interpretation of it. Thus, movement and rupture in *Jacques le Fataliste* are essential. The course of the action is literally and figuratively ambulatory, rambling, meandering, and jumbled. Circularity overlays the submerged linear movement of the main thread of Jacques' journey and love affair. The episodes need not occur in the order in which they do occur, but depend on the creator's arbitrary will, a metaphor for contingency and chance. Each is meaningful in itself, a different mirror of the same reality. Movement is anti-movement; meaning conveys the ultimate lack of meaning.[16] We have the aesthetic paradox of complex structure, embodying and illustrating the principles of disorder and instability.

Diderot's aesthetic theory is centered on the idea of relationships, on the creator's accomplishment of a structure that is intrinsically satisfying to the receptor, one that must also, to achieve full value, be satisfying in its communication of meaning and emotion. Art is the conscious process of seeking viable form, precisely as the cosmos is such an unconscious process. However, the meaning of form is quite different, not only because of self-conscious purpose, but because aesthetic form contains value—and a plurality of values. Art's unique attribute, which does not exist in any other aspect of known processes in the cosmos, is that in it human control makes possible an order eminently satisfactory to the mind.

Art may thus be considered as man's effort to conquer and overcome the universal law of transient forms, of construction and destruction. Here again it is unique.

[16] I am indebted to Professor John Kronik for the general formulations in this paragraph.

In nature and in all other spheres of human action, there is no escape from that law. Aesthetic structure, however, unlike others, does not disintegrate.[17] Although it is subject to the vagaries of taste and appreciation, in art alone man can defy the dissolution of form and win immortality within a limited yet vast cycle of time, despite the dissolution of his own structure. The necessary fictions of art are man's assertions against increasing entropy, against a blind and valueless "mechanical" universe, against the contingency and alienation of his cosmic status. But all this can only be within the microcosmic level of the species, which is one little configuration of the solar system (Diderot knew nothing of galaxies), which itself is one tiny fold in the seas of time. Pascal, on thinking of this, would have experienced a cosmic shudder. Diderot experienced no *frisson* of cosmic alienation, but he had a clear-sighted, luminous intellectual perception of it. Trilling goes too far: "For Diderot, the silence of the infinite spaces is not frightening; it is not even heard. For Diderot society is all in all the root and ground of alienation."[18] Society, though it is for Diderot the ground of alienation, is also the ground of accomplishment, and our only ground. He did not rebel against the human condition, but accepted it as the one within which we have to work and live. At least there were the joys of sex and social life, of doing good to others, of speculation and the aesthetic experience: "le bon, le vrai, et le beau."

Can we summarize what, in Diderot's mind, "the human condition" is? It will be useful for us to recog-

[17] One might say the same of mathematical structures, but these do not have the same physical presence or reality.

[18] *Sincerity and Authenticity*, p. 30.

nize his overall view, for he did have one clearly in mind, even though he never set it down in systematic form.

The human existential situation begins with the fact of a world beyond rational control and beyond rational explanation. The struggle for order against the contrary forces of disorder is universal. But if men are a part of that universal law of process, their self-awareness and consequent moral dimensionality make them accomplices in disorder, and fomenters of it. Utopian dreams are excluded: "Let us then accept things as they are," Moi suggests in *Le Neveu de Rameau.*[19] However, this attitude is not equivalent to apathy. Diderot is a man of the Enlightenment, a meliorist, and a reformer within the limits of the possible, limits that are both intrinsic to reality and a function of the antithetical forces at play.

Let us review the major limiting factors. First, the actions of others are beyond our control. They are frequently irrational and unpredictable. His protagonists undergo changes of fortune beyond their power to command, heedless of their consent. Our judgments of their actions and motives are wrong. The cruel judge in *Les Deux Amis de Bourbonne,* Gardeil, Mme. Reymer, Mme. de la Pommeraye—to cite a few instances—are really not understandable. Of the last, the master says, "Elle est incompréhensible."[20] She is a force, like a powerful wind or an earthquake, that nothing can halt.

Second, we frequently cannot exercise rational control over our own impulses and actions, and we do not control our destiny. "But in heaven's name, Author,

[19] *Le Neveu de Rameau,* p. 15.

[20] *Oeuvres romanesques,* p. 644.

you say to me, where were they going? But in heaven's name, Reader, I shall answer you, do we know where we are going? And you, where are you going?"[21] Diderot cannot control his thoughts—his "whores." Lui has impulses he cannot predict or explain. Jacques' "why's," like Zadig's, have no answer. Gardeil cannot explain his own actions,[22] and Diderot concludes his tale by moralizing: "one has neither the power of halting a passion that is enkindled, nor of prolonging one that is dying."[23] "Let us leave," Mlle. de la Chaux says with final resignation; "let us leave quickly; I cannot answer for what I would do or what I would say."[24] And this is Diderot's own comment:

> Let us pity men greatly, and blame them temperately. Let us look on the years gone by as so many moments in which we have escaped the wickedness that pursues us. And let us never think without shuddering of the violence of certain natural attractions. . . . The spark that chances to fall on a barrel of powder does not produce a more frightening effect. The finger that is ready to shake that fatal spark on you or on me is perhaps already raised.[25]

The image of the finger is not dissimilar from Jacques' capricious, "It was written up there."

Third, the natural law of self-interest, and its peculiarly human forms of satisfaction—superiority and domination over others—are the human reaction to existential contingency and the intuition of human disorder. If Diderot does not use these words, the ideas and feelings are omnipresent. Rousseau had said, "The wicked man orders everything in relation to himself."

[21] Ibid., p. 557. [22] Ibid., p. 805. [23] Ibid., p. 812.
[24] Ibid., p. 808. [25] Ibid., pp. 801-802.

The same idea is illustrated by Lui and many of Diderot's fictional characters. However, for him this is not always or necessarily the act of wickedness. Our natural impulse is to put order into our lives, to protect ourselves against the similar enterprise of others who wish to impose their own "order." The result is a general disorder. We recall the conclusion of the *Eléments de physiologie*: "The world is the house of the strong." Diderot never lets us forget it. "Let us look on the years gone by as so many moments in which we have escaped the wickedness that pursues us."

Diderot's view of the human comedy, or drama, is evidenced by his constant return to the master-slave theme. It winds its way throughout *La Religieuse*, *Ceci n'est pas un conte*, *Le Neveu de Rameau*, and not least *Jacques le Fataliste*. Between Jacques and his master there is a constant ambiguity and versatility of roles. Their unending joust forms a context for other patterns of mastery and servitude. Mme. de la Pommeraye had been her lover's slave: "she had submitted to all his fantasies, all his tastes; to please him, she had upset the plan of her life."[26] To secure her revenge, she will enslave two other women, use them as her instruments: "But above all, submissiveness, absolute, unlimited submissiveness to my will."[27] The result is intended to be a godlike, or rather a satanic, control over the destiny of her lover, Des Arcis. The Chevalier, an evil exploiter like the moral anarchist in "Droit naturel," warns Jacques: "Do you want to be the master or the slave, and the most abused of slaves?"[28] The tale of Father Hudson is the counterpart of that of Mme. de la Pommeraye. Even Mme. de la Carlière cannot help thinking

[26] Ibid., p. 652. [27] Ibid., p. 619. [28] Ibid., p. 734.

in the same categories: "the fresh memory of the suffering she had endured under a first husband's tyranny."[29] And she goes on to tell her suitor: "I am going to become the mistress of your happiness or unhappiness; you, the master of mine."

This is the intrinsic nature of human relationships, of our interdependency. It is twice generalized in *Jacques le Fataliste*. The first time by the narrator: "But who was the master of Jacques' master?—Come, do we lack masters in this world? Jacques' master had a hundred for one, like you."[30] And a second time by Jacques himself, in the more telling image of the dogs, which is only another rendition of Lui's "pantomime des gueux," or the figures of the "positions de Noverre."[31]

There is obviously a direct relation between Diderot's conceptualization of human drives and relationships and his picture of our world as one of disorder, largely of our own making. The problem of a rational moral life appears in ever darker hues and more insolvable riddles. In some cases—Mme. de la Pommeraye, Mme. de la Carlière—both master and slave are destroyed. Only Jacques and his master approach a solution, or more exactly, a *modus vivendi*. They transcend the master-slave relationship by recognizing it. They work out, through a rational dialogue between reasonable men, a combination of interdependence and freedom, one of mutual support in life's aimless and unpredictable journey. They go through a process of negotiation: "Let us stipulate."[32] Jacques will remain subservient, but the Master will tolerate his insolence. They will allow each other what will inevitably happen anyway.

Such a solution seems rare enough, though in life it is

[29] Ibid., p. 817.
[30] Ibid., pp. 537-38.
[31] Ibid., pp. 667-68.
[32] Ibid., p. 665.

undoubtedly more common than Diderot makes it appear. Similarly, he recognizes our potentiality for altruistic acts, in *Jacques le Fataliste* and *Les Deux Amis de Bourbonne,* but too often questions or denies their value. They are vain gestures, reflecting our longing for a world of moral order, destined to be engulfed in the more general disorder. Diderot's last play, *Est-il bon? Est-il méchant?* (1781) tells us that there may be no way of translating ideals into action except by means that contradict them. As we experience life, it is not an orderly pattern of cause and effect, but a chance concatenation of events that defies our notions of logic and necessity. It is never really intelligible—except in terms of Diderot's calculated aesthetic plan. If this is a logical and ordered world, one that "makes sense," then these qualities are hidden from our sight. *Jacques le Fataliste* begins and ends with an emphasis on "le hasard." This is our experience, and perhaps all we can know.[33]

If domination on an interpersonal level is destructive, it is still more so in the government of men. The freedom, dialogue, and contentious give-and-take exemplified by Jacques and his master are even more valuable in the realm of political life.

The movement of ideas we call the Enlightenment conceived its task as the release of men from error and prejudice—forms of disorder—and as the achievement of truth and human welfare—forms of order. With intellectual courage and clear-sightedness, Diderot saw

[33] For a contrary view, see G. May, "Le Maître, la chaîne et le chien dans *Jacques le Fataliste,*" *Cahiers de l'Association internationale des études françaises,* No. 13, 1961, pp. 269-82.

such efforts in a universal or cosmic context. Subject to the laws he understood to govern all being and all activity, they could not escape a fate common to all. The basic paradox of the universe as an anarchic order is the paradigm of all else. He understood, as Jean-Paul Sartre was to put it, that "the ordered world hid intolerable disorders," and that the world of explanations and reasons is not the world of existence.[34]

Throughout the universe, a meaningless game is being played. Convolutions of matter are blindly seeking stable structure. This *conatus* to persist in viability, and the eventual, inevitable dissolution, are parts of a deeper, more baffling cosmic process, the tendency to evolve ever more complex structures and "higher" levels of being. Life, species, and finally the self-conscious individual—these are the significant gradations of being.

If one looks beyond varying states of particular configurations to the all-encompassing whole, the universe is at any time in a state of equilibrium. Some structures are being formed, others broken down; but the overall situation remains the same. The same truth applies to man. He is engaged in a continuing struggle, but always (except in art) a losing one—as an individual and eventually as a species. He is enmeshed in the unique forms of intercourse that create the fabric of culture, which in turn struggles endlessly to establish moral and political structures capable of surviving the insolvable stresses between it and nature.

Diderot is often called a contradictory genius.[35] We have seen, however, that contradiction is the essence

[34] J.-P. Sartre, *Les Mots*, Paris, 1963, p. 66.

[35] See Ellen Strenski's useful summary, "The Problem of Inconsistency, Illustrated in Diderot's Social and Political Thought," in *Diderot Studies XIV*, pp. 197-216.

of reality. Order and disorder are the complementary qualities of the same reality. This truth he has understood, explored, and applied. In this regard there is fundamental consistency in his attitude and his approach to the operations of the world and of man. His philosophy is humanistic, man-centered. It suffers technically from the lack of a radical critique of his postulates and suppositions, such as we find in Hume. But he has properly apprehended man's place in the order of things, entirely a part of nature, yet unique in his way of being. Each level of structure brings into existence new kinds of law or process; but the lower levels are not abolished thereby. Man stands by himself, on the summit of the entire structure, with triumphs and problems that are his alone. He, too, is the creator of orders and the fomenter of disorders, but in his own way. The work of his reason is to create viable forms, to impose a novel order of culture upon the order of nature, and to suffer, as he alone can suffer, from his failures and frustrations. For him alone, "there are tears for things and mortal woes touch the mind."

Bibliography

Alexander, Ian. "Philosophy of Organism and Philosophy of Consciousness in Diderot's Speculative Thought," in *Studies in Romance Philosophy and French Literature presented to John Orr*, Manchester, 1953, pp. 1-21.

Basney, Lionel. "*Lucidus Ordo*. Johnson and Generality," *Eighteenth Century Studies*, vol. 5 (1971), pp. 39-57.

Becker, Carl. *The Heavenly City of the Eighteenth Century Philosophers*, New Haven, 1932.

Benot, Yves. *Diderot, de l'athéisme à l'anticolonialisme*, Paris, 1970.

Besse, Guy. "Observations sur la *Réfutation d'Helvétius* de Diderot," *Diderot Studies VI*, Genève, 1964, pp. 29-45.

Cartwright, M. T. *Diderot critique d'art et le problème de l'expression. Diderot Studies XIII*, Genève, 1969.

Charron, Jean. *Cosmology. Theories of the Universe*, London, 1970.

Crocker, L. G. *An Age of Crisis. Man and World in Eighteenth Century French Thought*, Baltimore, 1959.

———. "Diderot and Eighteenth Century French Transformism," in *Forerunners of Darwin*, Baltimore, 1959, Chapter V.

———. "*Jacques le Fataliste*, an *expérience morale*," *Diderot Studies III*, Genève, 1961, pp. 73-99.

———. "*Le Neveu de Rameau,* une expérience morale," *Cahiers de l'Association internationale des Etudes françaises,* pp. 133-56.

———. *Nature and Culture. Ethical Thought in Eighteenth Century France,* Baltimore, 1963.

———. *Rousseau's Social Contract. An Interpretive Essay,* Cleveland, 1968.

———. "Saint-Hyacinthe et le nihilisme moral," *Revue d'Histoire littéraire de la France,* vol. 64 (1964), pp. 462-66.

———. *Two Diderot Studies,* Baltimore, 1952.

Darnton, Robert. "The High Enlightenment and the Low-life of Literature in Pre-Revolutionary France," *Past and Present,* No. 51 (1971), pp. 81-115.

Diderot, Denis. *Commentaire sur la "Lettre sur l'homme et ses rapports" d'Hemsterhuis,* in *Oeuvres complètes,* ed. Roger Lewinter, Paris, 1971, vol. XI.

———. *Correspondance,* ed. G. Roth [and J. Varloot], Paris, 1955-1970, 16 vols.

———. *Eléments de physiologie,* édition critique par Jean Mayer, Paris, 1964.

———. *Le Neveu de Rameau,* édition critique par Jean Fabre, Genève et Lille, 1950.

———. *Le Rêve de d'Alembert,* ed. Jean Varloot, Paris, 1962.

———. *Lettre sur les sourds et muets.* Critical ed. by Paul H. Meyer, *Diderot Studies VII,* Genève, 1965.

———. *Oeuvres complètes,* ed. Assezat-Tourneux, Paris, 1875-77, 20 vols.

———. *Oeuvres esthétiques,* ed. Paul Vernière, Paris [1959].

———. *Oeuvres philosophiques,* ed. Paul Vernière, Paris [1956].

Diderot, Denis. *Oeuvres politiques*, ed. Paul Vernière, Paris, 1963.

———. *Oeuvres romanesques*, ed. Henri Bénac, Paris, 1962.

———. *Quatre contes*, ed. Jacques Proust, Genève, 1964.

Dieckmann, Herbert. *Cinq leçons sur Diderot*, Genève, 1959.

Doolittle, James. *Rameau's Nephew. A Study of Diderot's "Second Satire."* Genève, 1960.

Grava, Arnolds. "Diderot and Recent Philosophical Trends," *Diderot Studies IV*, Genève, 1963, pp. 73-104.

Grimsley, Ronald. "L'ambigüité dans l'oeuvre romanesque de Diderot," *Cahiers de l'Association internationale des Etudes françaises*, No. 13, Paris, 1961, pp. 223-37.

Hampshire, Stuart. Review of John Rawls' *A Theory of Justice, New York Review of Books*, February 24, 1972, pp. 34-39.

Jauch, J. M. *Are Quanta Real? A Galilean Dialogue*, Bloomington and London, 1973.

Kabelac, S. L. "Irony as a Metaphysics in *Le Neveu de Rameau*," *Diderot Studies XIV*, Genève, 1971, pp. 97-112.

Kiernan, Colm. "Additional Reflections on Diderot and Science," *Diderot Studies XIV*, Genève, 1971, pp. 113-142.

Lough, John. *Essays on the "Encyclopédie" of Diderot and d'Alembert*, London, 1968.

Manuel, F. E. and F. P. "Sketch for a Natural History of Paradise," *Daedalus*, vol. 101 (1972), pp. 83-128.

May, Georges. *Diderot et "La Religieuse."* New Haven and Paris, 1951.

———. "Le Maître, la chaîne et le chien dans *Jacques le Fataliste*," *Cahiers de l'Association internationale des Etudes françaises*, No. 13, 1961, pp. 269-82.

Monod, Jacques. *Chance and Necessity. An Essay on the Natural Philosophy of Modern Biology*, New York, 1972.

Mortier, Roland. "Diderot anti-colonialiste," *Revue belge de philologie et d'histoire*, vol. XLIX (1971), pp. 892-901.

Mauzi, Robert. "Diderot et le bonheur," *Diderot Studies III*, Genève, 1961, pp. 263-84.

Niklaus, Robert. *A Literary History of France. The Eighteenth Century. 1715-1789*. London and New York, 1970.

O'Gorman, Donal. *Diderot the Satirist*, Toronto, 1971.

Perkins, Jean. *The Concept of the Self in the French Enlightenment*. Genève, 1969.

Proust, Jacques. *Diderot et l'Encyclopédie*. Paris, 1962.

———. "Nouvelles recherches sur *La Religieuse*," *Diderot Studies VI*, Genève, 1964, pp. 197-214.

Roger, Jacques, "Diderot et Buffon en 1749," *Diderot Studies IV*, Genève, 1963, pp. 221-37.

Rousseau. *The Political Writings of Jean Jacques Rousseau*, ed. C. E. Vaughan, Cambridge, 1915, 2 vols.

Sartre, J.-P. *Les Mots*, Paris, 1963.

Strenski, Ellen. "The Problem of Inconsistency, Illustrated in Diderot's Social and Political Thought," *Diderot Studies XIV*, Genève, 1971, pp. 197-216.

Trilling, Lionel. *Sincerity and Authenticity*, New York, 1973.

Vartanian, Aram. "Erotisme et philosophie chez Diderot," *Cahiers de l'Association internationale des Etudes françaises*, No. 13, Paris, 1961, pp. 367-90.

Voltaire. *Traité de métaphysique,* ed. H. Temple Patterson, Manchester, 1937.

Waldauer, J. L. *Society and Freedom of the Creative Man in Diderot's Thought. Diderot Studies V,* Genève, 1964.

Wilson, A. M. "The Development and Scope of Diderot's Political Thought," in *Studies on Voltaire and the Eighteenth Century,* vol. XXVII (1963), pp. 1871-1900.

Index

INDEX

LIBRARY OF CONGRESS CATALOGING IN PUBLICATION DATA

Crocker, Lester G.
Diderot's chaotic order; approach to synthesis
Bibliography: p.
1. Diderot, Denis, 1713-1784. I. Title.
B2017.C74 194 73-22127
ISBN 0-691-07199-3

Lightning Source UK Ltd.
Milton Keynes UK
UKHW020954011122
411452UK00006B/490